Our Debt to Greece and Rome

George Depue Hadzsits, Ph.D.

David Moore Robinson, Ph.D., LL.D.

GREEK AND ROMAN
FOLKLORE

BY
WILLIAM REGINALD HALLIDAY, B.A., B.Litt.

COOPER SQUARE PUBLISHERS, INC.
NEW YORK
1963

Published 1963 by Cooper Square Publishers, Inc.
59 Fourth Avenue, New York 3, N. Y.
Library of Congress Catalog Card No. 63-10289

To

E. H. H.

WHO KNOWS HOW FAIRY TALES SHOULD END

Nam, ut vere loquamur, superstitio fusa per gentis
oppressit omnium fere animos atque hominum
inbecillitatem occupavit.   Cic., *De Div.*, II. 148.

PREFACE

SOME critic whose patience carries him to the end of the third chapter, may possibly be reminded of the chapter of Dr. Horrebow's *Natural History of Iceland* to which Dr. Johnson has given fame. " Chapter LXXII, Concerning Snakes," was its title: its contents were as follows: — " There are no snakes to be met with throughout the whole island." But it is the purpose of this series not to exaggerate, but to assess a debt. And if the European superstitions and folktales which can be said with certainty to have been invented by classical antiquity and thence to have been transmitted direct to the modern world, are few, the common property of modern and ancient folklore is shown to be considerable. Here we may mention that the mutual debt of the studies of Greek and Roman religion on the one hand, and of European folklore on the other, is incalculable.

My statements of fact must be taken on trust. I early came to the conclusion that the piling up of references in a little essay of this character was useless pedantry, and though the actual illustrations used are mainly derived from my own miscellaneous reading, the matters which they illustrate are fairly typical and well known. With regard to references to classical authors, I soon found that in practice all must be given or none; I have therefore contented myself with generally indicating the kind of authority for specific statements by " Pliny says," " we learn from Aristophanes," or some similar phrase. The few references which are given in the notes are intended to supplement the information in the text by indicating where further detail, which considerations of scale did not allow me to give, may be found. In the chapter on *Folktales* I have habitually quoted the numbers of the variants in Grimm. This will enable the reader to refer also to the great dictionary of variants, Bolte and Polívka, *Anmerkungen zu den Kinder- und Hausmärchen der Brüder Grimm,* of which the long delayed index volume is not yet to hand. For Aesop's *Fables* I have used the numeration of the standard Greek text of Halm.

Finally the purpose of the intrusive personal

pronoun, where it occurs, is intended to help the reader to discriminate between my personal views and those which have the more considerable sanction of received opinion.

CONTENTS

[xi]

GREEK AND ROMAN
FOLKLORE

GREEK AND ROMAN FOLKLORE

I. INTRODUCTORY

THE study of folklore is concerned with survivals. It embraces the superstitions, festivals, customs, and amusements (games, songs, stories, riddles, and proverbs) of the less sophisticated portion of the community. The sanction for the continued existence or practice of these is primarily that of tradition. The old favorite stories or recipes have been passed down from father to son or from mother to daughter; beyond the memory of the oldest inhabitant and, from what his grandfather told him, for time out of mind the village has observed such and such a custom upon a stated anniversary. The appeal is to what the Romans called *mos maiorum,* the custom of the ancestors, the inherited experience of the race.

[3]

The conservatism of simple folk is extraordinarily tenacious. A number of the beliefs, customs, or ideas which in this way have become embalmed in popular tradition, have survived from immemorial antiquity. They are found not only among the peasantry of Europe but also among the less highly developed races in all parts of the world. For instance the idea that the imitation of a natural process will magically produce it, that thunder can be induced by making a noise like thunder, that rain can be summoned by sprinkling water, or that the fertility of fields or flocks can be promoted by the performance of the sexual act, may be said to find universal expression. Universal again may be called the belief in an external soul, that is to say the existence of some external object with the safety of which the life of an individual is bound up, or the conviction that a man's health and well-being may be affected by the treatment of some part of his person — his portrait or effigy, a lock of his hair, or his nail-clippings. The existence of these and similar ideas has been observed among all peoples at a certain stage of culture, and though from time to time the attempt is made to derive all cultural elements from some

[4]

single source, from ancient Egypt or from a lost Atlantis, the contention of Tylor and the earlier anthropologists remains in my opinion unshaken, viz., that at a certain stage of intellectual and social development the human mind reacts to similar circumstances in similar ways. A number of simple general ideas of this kind, which are, after all, psychologically intelligible, must have been developed independently in different places. They are rooted in human nature. Neither the place nor date of their origin can be determined. Whenever or wherever people have attained a certain level of civilization, they are observed to occur.

Obviously, however, the whole content of popular tradition does not belong to so dim and distant a past. There is no valley so sequestered nor island set in so remote a sea as to provide the opportunity for a community of human beings to maintain its existence in complete isolation from cultural contacts of any kind. Nor in any civilized society has there ever been a gulf so great between the classes, that the more backward element in the community has remained wholly uninfluenced by the ideas of the more sophisticated element. For a community is in fact a continuous unit. The rate of infiltration from top to bottom under certain conditions may be very slow and partial in effect, but it must always be operative. Besides, therefore, the element to which no origin nor date can be assigned, we shall necessarily expect to discover matters which have been transmitted from an alien source, or cases where the learned tradition of an earlier generation has contributed to popular beliefs, customs, and literature, if for convenience we may use this term of matter which is primarily handed down not by letters but by word of mouth.

In particular cases it is often very difficult to be sure as to whether a specific phenomenon is due to transmission or to independent original invention. Let me give an example of a problem to which I should be very unwilling to give a dogmatic answer. The Romans employed the practice of examining the liver of the victim of sacrifice for omens. That they learned this from the Etruscans we know for certain. It is generally held that the Etruscans in turn had learned it before they came to Italy probably from Asia Minor (somewhere about the beginning of the eighth century B.C.), and that they had borrowed it from the civilization of Mesopotamia, where it was also elaborated. I am myself more inclined .owards the probability of this view than I once was, though there remains, I notice, a considerable geographical gap between the Mesopotamian kingdoms and any probable Eastern home of the Etruscans. But it is not inconceivable that the art was an independent invention of the Etruscans, for the practice of examining the liver of an animal which is killed for sacrifice or for some important domestic festival, is fairly common, and it has been observed among peasantry who have no obvious links with Etruria or Mesopotamia. A natural anxiety is aroused by solemn moments like those of sacrifice, which tends to attribute significance to any abnormality which attends the performance. The liver is a remarkable organ and noticeably variable in its outward appearance, while it is also very generally considered to be the seat of the intelligence or of the emotions. No doubt for these reasons it is not infrequently the object of special attention upon such occasions. Either solution therefore is quite possible. It is not inconceivable that the Etruscans learned to interpret the signs upon the livers of sacrificial victims, from the Babylonians, but it is equally possible that the elabo-

rate art developed independently, from a sim
lar simple omen-taking, in each of the tw
areas.

Another case happens to be easier to decide
It is a very remarkable fact that the native
of Borneo practice a system of divination by
birds which presents a strikingly close analogy
to ancient Italic augury. But here the difficulty
of constructing any intermediate links by
which the ancient Italians could have transmitted this practice to remote Borneo must
surely be decisive for the probability that the
similarity of custom is due to a coincidence of
independent invention.

The student of folklore, therefore, will always be on the alert to discriminate between
elements which are rooted in human nature
and are probably of very ancient and native
origin within the area which he is considering,
and elements which have either been borrowed
from alien sources or are the relatively recent
product of the learned tradition of an earlier
generation. The problem, it will be seen, is not
always an easy one, but to remember its existence is salutary. There is perhaps no branch of
learned enquiry in which wild speculations are
so rashly offered and accepted as in the study of

folklore. Whenever we are told that some particular phenomenon carries us back to the mental
or physical habits of palaeolithic man or that it
proves the transmission of culture from the
VIth Dynasty in Egypt, we need to examine
the probabilities very carefully in the light (a)
of what we know of its distribution among the
later human societies and (b) of what little we
know of the palaeolithic age or of ancient
Egyptian culture as the case may be, distinguishing here very carefully between ascer-
tained facts and arbitrary subjective interpretations, which have been put upon them.

An essay of this kind cannot, of course, attempt an exhaustive examination of the folklore of ancient Greece and Italy. The most it
can profitably aim at doing is first of all to
illustrate by some examples the character of
the folklore elements in classical culture, phenomena that is to say which were already survivals in the Greek and Roman civilizations.
Secondly we must attempt some discussion of
the relation of the legends, mythology, and
fables of the Greeks and Romans to the folktales of the Indo-European area. Thirdly we
must consider the effect which was produced
upon the imagination and hence upon the pop-

ular ideas of Europe by the grandeur of the Graeco-Roman civilization, and the degree to which the learning of the later classical epoch contributed to the subsequent vulgar superstitions of Europe.

Our debt specifically to Greece and Rome in these matters is not perhaps so large, as it is certainly not so important, as in things of greater value. The superstitions and customs, which we must consider in our first section, have their parallels in European folklore, but their presence there may not be due to direct inheritance from their classical analogues. In the main they are part of the common stock of ideas belonging to the relatively low stages of human development. As regards folktales the result of our investigations are likely to be mainly negative; here we cannot neglect the important problems of the relation of classical to oriental stories. The intellectual and scientific tradition of medieval Europe, which will engage us in the third section, may at least bring home to us the continuity of European culture and show how multiple, close, and intimate are the ties which even in trivial things bind us to the Greeks and Romans.

Before going further, it may perhaps be

worth while to remind ourselves of the general course of that tradition. Between the years 1000 and 500 B.C. the Greeks created a new civilization in the Eastern Mediterranean. Characteristic of this people was an intense love of independence, a restless and insatiable curiosity, a very high degree of aesthetic and intellectual sensibility, and a remarkable power of analysis and generalization, which led them to look behind particular phenomena for the general principles which govern their manifestation. It was this last capacity which enabled the Greeks to take over the patiently accumulated experience of the older civilizations and to create therefrom the sciences. Thus the necessity imposed by the annual inundations of the Nile had taught the Egyptians the empirical art of land measurement, but it was the Greeks who discovered geometry; the Babylonians had for centuries recorded the movements of the heavenly bodies, but the Greeks invented the principles of astronomy. Scientific investigation in a true sense was born with the Greeks.

The natural qualities of the Greek race were, no doubt, intensified by the peculiarity of their political organization in a number of independent city-states, the very small scale of which promoted an extraordinary degree of energy and activity in political and intellectual life. The city-state was the forcing frame of Greek talent. At the turn of the sixth and fifth centuries B.C. Hellenism came into collision with a great organized oriental state, Persia. The Greek cities of the Asia Minor coast, which had hitherto led the van in intellectual and artistic achievement, were conquered, and Greece itself was invaded. A temporary combination of patriotic cities succeeded in repelling the invader, but two results of the conflict followed. The center of Hellenic culture passed from the eastern Greeks to Athens, and the inexorable logic of events had shown that if Hellenism in its existing form was to preserve its independent existence, the formation of some larger and more powerful political unit than the city-state was necessary. But for this to be successfully accomplished, a subordination of individual liberties was required which the fierce love of independence of the city-state was unable to endure. The attempt to establish an Athenian maritime empire led, in the latter half of the fifth century, to a long war in which the whole Greek-speaking world

became involved; the result was the disruption
of the Athenian empire and the exhaustion of
the Greek world. War did not end war, but left
a legacy of quarrelsomeness, increasingly futile
but increasingly ineradicable as the resources
of the individual Greek states became weaker
and weaker. The disintegration of the Greek
world was then arrested in the latter half of
the fourth century by the Macedonians, Philip
and Alexander, who constituted themselves the
champions of Hellenism, in effect destroyed the
independence of the Greek city-state, and dealt
finally with the menace of Persia. Having conquered the East as far as the Punjab, Alexander died, a young man, leaving no adult heir
to complete his work. His empire split up
into three great rival monarchies, which
between them controlled the Eastern Mediterranean.

Alexander's conquests profoundly affected
the current of civilization. He had been the
champion of Hellenism, and Greek was the
official language spoken throughout the kingdoms of his Successors. Greek culture remained the dominant element which gave its
form to the civilization which is called Hellenistic. For though in many respects profoundly

Greek, it was no longer purely Greek. Alexander had carried Hellenism into the East, but the East had inevitably reacted upon Hellenism. The true center of the Eastern Mediterranean culture now passed from Athens to Alexandria in Egypt, the greatest of Alexander's foundations.

In the meantime in Italy a single people, the Romans, had patiently fought their way to power. Rather unimaginative, but richly endowed with the military qualities of discipline, patriotism, courage, and tenacity, and gifted with a genius for practical affairs, they gradually mastered the Italian peninsula. In very early times they had been influenced by the Greek colonies in Southern Italy, which were then independent neighbours. Their alphabet, for example, was derived from Greek Cumae, and already before the fall of the monarchy, Greek religion had begun to affect that of the Romans. In religion Greek influences became increasingly prominent, and eventually the Greek pantheon and Greek mythology were bodily taken over by Rome. Roman literature, again, begins with the translation of Homer into Latin by a Greek slave, who was captured in 272 B.C., when the fall of Tarentum made the Greek cities of Italy subjects of Rome. Roman civilization and literature were therefore almost from the first derivative, and their Greek character was naturally intensified by direct contact with and the subsequent conquest of Greece itself. In consequence it is very difficult to distinguish genuinely Italic beliefs, stories, or superstitions from the superimposed Greek borrowings, and for the purposes of this essay we shall for the most part treat the Graeco-Roman civilization as a single unit.

Eventually Rome conquered the whole seaboard of the Mediterranean and a large part of Western Europe. To the ruder peoples of the west she gave their civilization, but this was essentially Graeco-Roman, a continuous development from the Hellenistic culture. For two centuries after the birth of Christ the Roman Empire gave the blessings of ordered government and peace to an area bounded upon the west by the Atlantic, on the north by the Rhine and Danube, on the east by the upper Euphrates and the Palestinian desert, and on the south by the sands of Libya and the Sahara. Throughout this area travel and commerce were free and active. As a result, the constant intercommunication of men and ideas created a single civilization which became increasingly homogeneous. Although Latin, not Greek, was the current language of the western half of the Empire, it was the eastern half which supplied the dominating cultural influence. In particular it was during these years of peace that a new religion, the form of which was characteristically Hellenistic (for if the Founder of Christianity was born in Judaea, His message was necessarily conveyed to the gentile world in the language of Greek philosophy), was striking deep roots in every part of the Roman world.

In the third century after Christ the decline of the Roman Empire had set in. From various causes its internal vitality had been impaired, and the external pressure on its frontiers had increased. For two centuries, though with difficulty, the barbarians were more or less kept out; then in the fifth century after Christ the Western Empire was overrun. Although the majesty of Rome was such that a world without a Roman empire was inconceivable even to the barbarian imagination, and the shadowy Holy Roman Empire was perpetuated until it finally vanished, an extremely attenuated ghost, almost within our own times, yet the shock

to the body politic which was administered by
the invasions of the fifth century, was too violent to be repaired, and the intrusive racial elements were too considerable to be assimilated
or absorbed into the old order. Gradually from
the ruins of the western empire there emerged
the great nations of Europe. But though this
process of differentiation was going on, although the spoken Latin was following different lines of local development to form the separate languages of Italy, France, and Spain, the
main current of civilization still flowed in a
single stream. Increasing political differentiation there was, with all its attendant conse-
quences, but nevertheless there were two forces
which gave a real unity to European civilization as a whole. In the first place the Roman
Empire, which finally collapsed, had been a
Christian Empire, and the authority of the
Church ran throughout western Christendom
irrespective of national boundaries. In the second place the knowledge accumulated by the
past was not entirely lost. The ancient language in which it was preserved was retained
by the Church and also by scholarship; Latin
remained for centuries an international tongue
spoken and written by men of education. In-

deed, ever since the Roman Empire, European scholarship has remained international; for before the almost complete disuse of Latin in favour of the vernaculars had raised new barriers to internationalism, the invention of printing had broken down others in compensation.

The tradition which flows from the ancient Greeks, through Hellenistic, Roman, and Medieval channels, to the modern world is then a single stream, but the swiftness of its current and the limpidity of its waters are not uniform along its course. The Greek genius in the period of the city-state was highly rational. Even in the sphere of religion, which upon the whole was very little mystical, the more primitive survivals tended to be pushed into the background. A change, however, begins in the Hellenistic period, and science becomes more and more infected with superstition. A number of causes, besides the oriental influences which we have noticed to be at work, assisted in producing this result. The sciences became the highly specialized preserves of experts. Simultaneously education was diffused over a wider area, but its quality was watered down in the process. Education by the inculcation of miscellane-

ous information provided by popular handbooks upon great subjects had its birth. With
the disappearance of the city-state, Greek intellectual power lost much of its dynamic and
creative force. Philosophy now became concerned rather to find a rule of happiness than
to discover truth in the spirit of disinterested
curiosity. Man's life was viewed against a
wider horizon, that of the individual's member-
ship in the physical universe rather than that of
his citizenship in a small political community.
The wider horizon, however, was purchased at
the price of sharpness of focus. The influence
of the East showed itself in a growing sense of
human weakness and sin, in a more uneasy
attitude towards Heaven and a future life, and
in a number of specific contributions, of which
the pseudo-science of astrology was one of the
most far-reaching and devastating in its results. Throughout the later classical antiquity
the force of rationalism declined in favour of
credulity. Whereas the interest of the earlier
Greeks had been to reject what did not stand
the test of reason, that of the later classical age
was to exalt the irrational, on the supposition
that it must conceal some hidden meaning.
" There must be something in it " expresses the

attitude of an age which began to spend ingenuity in finding reasons to believe the in-
credible.

This attitude of mind led to a great revival
of the primitive survivals to which the Greeks
of the classical age, even if their conservatism
had retained them, had paid but little attention. Both philosophy and science became infected with the new credulity and reassumed
garments which had been discarded in their
vigorous youth. The demonology of Neo-Platonism helped to rivet upon Christendom the
belief in the incessant intervention of good and
evil spirits in the ordinary affairs of life and to
make real the terrors of witchcraft and the
magician's art. Science, having abandoned the
touchstone of reason, became indiscriminate in
its erudition. Medicine became as much concerned with 'possession' or with magical remedies as with the investigation of natural
causes. Here we may contrast the temper of
Hippocrates in the fifth century B.C., who
stoutly maintained that epilepsy could not be
simply the unavoidable result of divine wrath
on the grounds that all diseases must have a
natural cause, with that of even the greatest
doctor of imperial times, Galen, who recom-

mends the suspension of a peony round the neck to cure this malady.

Now it is in its late classical form that the intellectual heritage of Greek and Roman civilization passed on into Europe. Thanks to this credulous temper, which we have noted, a large number of revived superstitions, to which the approval of learning had lent a new dignity, were transmitted with the sanction of authority to medieval science. Just as in the case of folktales we shall notice how a concurrent literary tradition helped to reinforce the chances of survival of oriental forms of stories, so, particularly as regards magical remedies, the written learned tradition reinforced the popularity of certain folklore beliefs. Indeed it is sometimes difficult to know whether a particular belief has its source in the genuinely popular tradition or has been introduced by infiltration from superstitious learning.

It is indeed to this revival of the superstitious attitude in the later classical period that a great deal of our information about Greek and Roman folklore is due. Books like the *Natural History* of the Elder Pliny collected a mass of information about magical remedies, pious students of religion like Plutarch were especially interested in the primitive elements in Greek religion which demanded philosophical explanation to justify their existence, even the archaelogists like Pausanias show a marked preference for the more curious and antique cults. Antiquaries of all kinds flourished in an uncreative age, and the antiquary is ever a genial Autolycus; all the unconsidered and inconsiderable trifles are grist to his mill. Thus the *Word Book* of Julius Pollux has preserved long lists of such details as children's games, and that extraordinary compilation *The Cook's Oracle* (*Deipnosophistae*) of Athenaeus contains a mass of information about every kind of curious detail of classical life.

A great deal, again, of what belongs properly to folklore is naturally to be discovered in religious belief and practice. For religious ritual in particular is exceptionally conservative, and ceremonies are often retained even when the worshippers have forgotten their original meaning or purpose. Here the modern investigator is assisted by analogies which are provided by the folklore of other peoples, and there can be little doubt, for instance, that we have a truer appreciation of the character of the earliest stratum of Roman religion today than Varro or Ovid had in the days of Julius Caesar and Augustus.

Our other sources of information are naturally capricious, depending as they do upon chance references in literature. This is inevitable. One might be well enough read in English literature without ever happening to have come across a reference to a Maypole or to Plough Monday. The sources in Greek and Roman literature which do provide us with random but valuable information, are just what we should expect. A philosopher may use a riddle or a childrens' game as an illustration, but the lion's share of incidental information will naturally be provided by realistic types of literature such as the Hellenistic studies of low life, sentimentalized as in most of Theocritus or treated with brutal realism as in the *Mimes* of Herodas, or the later picaresque novels like the *Satiricon* of Petronius and the *Metamorphoses* of Apuleius. True satire, again, is inevitably fruitful in allusions to the trivialities and superstitions of every day life, and a great deal is to be learned from Horace, Persius, and Juvenal.

In conclusion I may mention one topic,

which is perhaps expected of me but which nevertheless I do not propose to handle, viz. the very difficult question of local and continuous survivals from the classical civilizations, in modern Greece and Italy respectively. The question is highly controversial, though its answer one way or the other is relatively unimportant. Some degree of survival no doubt there may well have been. We may agree, for example, with Warde Fowler's comment on the inherited Italian instinct for processional ritual, which was characteristic of Roman religion in its earliest days. " The stately processions remained, and could be watched with pride by the patriotic Roman all through the period of the Empire, until the Roman Church adapted them to its own ritual and gave them, as we saw, a new meaning. As the cloud shadows still move slowly over the hollows of the Apennines, so does the procession of the patron saint pass still through the streets of many an Italian city." But, as a general rule, the natural sentiment of classical scholars and, where they happen to be Greeks or Italians, a wholly admirable jealousy for their birth-right in a glorious past, may be thought unduly to load the scales. Is it really probable, for instance,

that the Carnival or Epiphany mumming plays
of modern Greece are necessarily lineal and direct descendants of Dionysiac ritual, when in
fact they present yet closer analogies to seasonal peasant practices in other parts of Europe? Or again, if, as is no doubt the case, the
name of the modern Greek Charos or Charon-
das is connected with the ancient name Charon,
does it amount to very much when the whole
conception of the figure is different? For
whereas Charon was the ferryman, who rowed
the souls across the river of the Lower World,
Charos is the ruthless, powerful, and ineluct-
able personification of Death. Often eagerness
has completely outrun discretion, as for example in the current statement that St. Elias,
whose chapels crown the hills of modern
Greece, has simply taken the place of Helios,
the ancient sun-god. The apparent phonetic
plausibility is a little discounted when the certain facts are recollected, that the cult of Helios
was actually of very restricted distribution in
antiquity, and that Zeus, not the sun-god, was
par excellence the god of hill tops.

Alleged local survivals in modern Greece
and Italy are therefore most safely to be ap-
proached in a somewhat critical spirit. That

some exist and can be established I have no doubt, but I am equally certain that a great number of alleged survivals will not stand critical examination. But neither the attempt to establish authentic instances, nor the labour of refuting popular errors in detail are appropriate to a book of this kind. I propose in consequence deliberately to set these particular problems on one side, and, as regards survival, to concentrate our attention not upon the folklore of modern Greece or Italy, but upon the relation of the classical civilizations to the folklore and the tradition of medieval and modern Europe.

II. SUPERSTITIOUS BELIEFS AND PRACTICES

TO COMPILE a complete list of the coincidences between classical and modern folklore would require not a chapter, but a larger volume than this. The following are illustrations only, which have been selected in order to give an idea of the range and nature of the similarities. Some may be due to direct transmission, but these are probably a small minority; for most of the superstitions enumerated are so general in their distribution that they may be thought to belong to the common property of the human intelligence at a certain stage of its development.

It may also be repeated that these phenomena were survivals in classical antiquity, just as their analogues are survivals with us. We may further remember with profit that though we talk in a superior way of the superstitions of the peasantry, there is not one of us who does not consciously or unconsciously indulge in some superstitious rite or formula almost every day of his life. The Elder Pliny's words hold good today. " There arises first of all one question, of the greatest importance and always attended with the same uncertainty, whether words, charms, and incantations are of any efficacy or not. . . . Though the wisest of our fellow men, I should remark, taken individually, refuse to place the slightest faith in these opinions, yet, in our every day life, we practically show, each passing hour, that we do entertain this belief, though at the moment we are not sensible of it."

The processes of birth, which in classical antiquity, as among mankind at large, were regarded with superstitious anxiety, would seem to provide an appropriate starting point for our survey. In Greece prophylactic herbs were placed in the bed of the expectant mother, whose labour it was feared might be retarded by magical means. Tying knots, sitting beside her with the fingers intertwined, or with one leg placed over the other were magical gestures which ill-disposed persons might employ to hinder easy delivery. These devices of sympathetic magic find numerous parallels elsewhere. As an example we may take the converse remedy for difficult labour among the Koita of New Guinea. If labour is unduly prolonged, the father is sent for. He *opens* any boxes there may be in the house, then sits down near his wife and *unties* the cord which confines his hair.

The Greek mother was for a period unclean, and the women who had assisted at the birth counted as such, until they were formally purified at the *amphidromia*, six days later. In places of great sanctity, for instance the holy island of Delos, which was sacred to Apollo, no birth might take place, and women must be removed from the island before their time came. Similarly among the Tlingit a birth must not take place in the family dwelling. A hole is dug behind the house inside a little hut or shelter, and here, regardless of the weather, the unfortunate mother must go for her confinement. The *Superstitious Man* in Theophrastus' *Characters* felt himself to be infected by pollution, if he so much as saw a woman who had recently been delivered.

After a birth the house door was painted with pitch from thorn bushes, which had the property of keeping evil spirits away, and a prophylactic wreath of olive branches (for a boy) or a fillet of wool (for a girl) was hung outside it as an amulet. On the sixth day after birth the *amphidromia* or *running round* took place, when the father decided whether the child was to be reared or to be exposed, as girl children sometimes were. The festival took its name from the rite of carrying the child round the family hearth. The original purpose of this action is a matter of dispute, and whether it was sought to bring the child into touch with the purifying strength of fire or to incorporate it as a member of the family by contact with the family hearth, or, as has also been suggested, to give it fleetness of foot, remains doubtful. But an interesting detail is the fact that the father ran round naked with the child, for both the magic circle and the nudity of the agent are very frequent features of magical ceremonies in all parts of the world. An interesting parallel in modern folk practice is the Esthonian custom, according to which the father runs round the church in which the child is being baptised. With reference to the hearth we may notice also the Irish christening rite mentioned below. (p. 33.)

At Rome too the period of birth was fraught with peril for mother and child. A candle was kept continuously burning in the room, as it is, for instance, in Modern Greece and Germany today, in order to give spiritual protection. After the birth had taken place three men armed with an axe, pestle, and broom respectively, swept and struck the threshold. The original object of this ritual was no doubt to sweep out any evil that might be in the house and to drive off any which might be attempting to come in. In historical times the axe was said to drive away Silvanus, the spirit of the forest. We might perhaps compare its use with the Polish peasant practice of laying an axe-head with the sharp edge outermost in the gateway of the home of a newly-married couple.

With regard to the use of the axe, its prophylactic virtue is due not merely to its character as an instrument of offence but also to the material of which it is made. To iron magical properties are often attributed, perhaps a reminiscence of the time when the metal was first introduced, and iron implements were regarded as strange, novel, magically efficient objects of wonder. Hence in modern Europe the iron horse-shoe upon the stable door will prevent the horses from being hag-ridden, and an iron axe-head upon the barrel of beer will prevent it turning sour in thunder. Somewhat similarly Pliny the Elder, who tells us that eggs are addled by thunder or spoiled by the cry of the hawk, recommends us to place an iron nail or a clod from the plough under the straw upon which the eggs lie in order to avert the danger from the thunder. The converse to this attribution of magical properties to iron is supplied by the *taboo* upon the strange metal, which was retained in some of the most ancient rituals of Roman religion. Thus, for example, the *Flamen Dialis*, holder of the most ancient priesthood of Jupiter, might not cut his hair nor his nails with an iron knife; the ploughshare used for tracing out the circuit of a colony must be of bronze not of iron; the use of an iron pruning-hook in the sacred grove of the Arval Brethren necessitated special piacular or disinfecting sacrifices; no iron might be used in the construction or repair of the *Pons Sublicius*, the oldest of Roman bridges. The witch, according to Virgil and Horace, must reap her magic herbs at midnight with a *bronze* sickle.

But we have been led to digress from our infant, who is still at a critical stage. The most anxious and dangerous time of all is, of course, the helpless period after birth, before the child has received, as it were, its human identity, i.e. before the *amphidromia* in Greece (though here the name was not conferred until a second family festival on the eighth or tenth day after birth) or at Rome before the *dies lustricus* upon the eighth (girls) or ninth day (boys). Similarly in English peasant belief a child "never thrives until it is christened," and it is during this dangerous period that the Irish mother dreads the removal of her child and the substitution of a changeling. In County Leitrim after a child was christened, a turf from the fire was quenched and a piece of it sewn on to the child's bib. After nine days it was taken off and sewn into a little bag with a cross worked upon the outside of it and placed under the child's pillow, to prevent it being overlooked. The chief terror of the classical mother was the *strix*, a vampire witch, who came by night to suck the blood of infants. The anaemic pallor of the child and perhaps the marks left by the witches' talons on its face might betray their dreadful work. A Greek fragment has survived of what is perhaps a nursery incantation " to send away the *strix*, the crier by night, from the land, the nameless bird, upon the swift ships." Ovid prescribes a more elaborate and perhaps more efficacious remedy. Door-posts and threshold are three times struck with boughs of arbutus and purifying water is sprinkled. Then a two-months-old porker is killed, and its entrails are declared to be a surrogate offering for the child; a life is offered for a life. The offering is then placed in the open air, and everyone who is present must be careful not to look back. Finally branches of prophylactic buckthorn are placed in the window of the room, just as Malays put thistles in the windows and doors to keep out the similar blood-sucking Penangal.

After the ceremony of the *dies lustricus* until the age of puberty the Roman boy wore the *toga praetexta*, a robe with a broad purple stripe, like that worn by the highest religious and secular functionaries, and, suspended round his neck, the *bulla*, a small circular box containing usually a representation of the male organ, a very frequent form of amulet against the evil eye in all parts of the world. The purpose of the amulet and of the purple stripe upon the garments, which were peculiar to childhood and to important political or religious office, was undoubtedly prophylactic. The young, like the 'tender lambs' of Virgil's shepherd, are peculiarly susceptible to being 'overlooked.' Children in Pliny's time wore coral amulets. "Coralls," comments the Caroline antiquary Aubrey, "are worne by children still: but in Ireland they value the fang-tooth (holder) of an wolfe before it; which they set in silver and gold as we doe ye Coralls." Personally I cut my teeth upon a peccary's tooth set in silver.

Persius describes how the old wives who are skilled in averting the "burning eye," spit on their middle finger and rub saliva upon the infant's forehead. Spitting as a countercharm is a folklore practice of universal distribution. Classical literature contains numbers of examples of spitting to avert the evil, when you see a maniac or an epileptic. In a German railway carriage I have myself been requested by a peasant woman to spit in the face of her husband, who happened to be seized with an epileptic fit. As regards the evil eye the sixth *Idyll* of Theocritus provides a good example. The love-sick Polyphemus, after looking at his reflection in the sea, persuades himself that he is not so hideous after all, nay positively good-looking. "Then to shun the evil eye did I spit thrice in my breast; for this spell was taught me by the crone, Cottytaris, that piped of yore to the reapers in Hippocoon's field." Polyphemus reminds us of the dangers of overt praise as inducing the evil eye of envy. Amongst any superstitious peasantry in Europe it is unwise to admire a child too explicitly, for that brings bad luck. Virgil's shepherds knew this too; their remedy against the danger was a wreath of berries. Frequently a mother will try to counteract the indiscreet admiration which may bring a nemesis, by some act or speech of disparagement, and this is perhaps why the granny of Persius, used her middle finger, the *digitus infamis*.

The legendary Telchines, the first metallurgists, were said to have possessed the power of the evil eye and to have been able to bring down rain and hail, as well as to blast the crops of their neighbours by a glance. The earliest Roman code of laws, the XII Tables, contained a provision against those who charmed away their neighbour's crop. The idea here seems to have been that it was possible by an incantation to transfer the fruitfulness of your neighbour's crop to your own, an explanation which, as C. Furius Cressimus complained, readily enough suggests itself to envious incompetence in order to account for the better farmer's better harvest. A sure sign that an individual possessed the evil eye was a double pupil. The Thibii of Pontus were notorious for this physical peculiarity and its concomitant magical power. Like the witches of Europe, if thrown into water, they were not submerged.

Marriage is everywhere a critical and therefore a dangerous moment in human life, when the evil eye and other hostile influences are to be feared. Among the preliminary rites of ancient Greek marriage was a ritual bath in water drawn for the purpose in a special kind of pitcher, usually from a particular local spring (e.g. in Athens from the fountain Kallirhoë or at Thebes from Ismenus). In modern Greece similarly a ritual bath in water from the local *hagiasma* or sacred spring is frequently a necessary prelude to marriage. With the ancient custom no doubt was connected the practice of placing upon the monuments of girls who died unmarried, a representation of a water jar of the kind which was employed in this rite. In the Troad we are told that girls before marriage waded into the river Scamander and formally offered to it their virginity. The association of rivers and water-powers with fertility and children is perhaps at the bottom of these customs. Rivers in ancient Greece were thought to nurture the growth of children (*kourotrophoi*), and it was the common practice for boys to dedicate to a river a lock of hair which was cut off and offered when they reached manhood or married. Of this the famous example of Achilles and the Spercheius may remind us.

The favorite time for Greek marriages was in the winter month *Gamelion* and at the full moon. In England it is still thought unlucky to be married in May, a month which the ancient Romans also eschewed, in part no doubt because the gloomy rites of the *Lemuria*, which are described below (p. 45), fell within it. In Boeotian weddings, when the bride was brought home to the bridegroom's house, a wheel of the chariot was burned, to signify, so Plutarch tells us, that her stay there was to be permanent. In Greece generally the bride's arrival was greeted with a shower of dates, cakes, dried figs, and nuts. I do not agree with the connection, which some scholars have seen, of these *katachusmata*, as they were called, with offerings to the dead. They were also showered upon a new household slave, and I should regard them merely as a charm to promote good luck and plenteous prosperity. We might compare our own practice of showering rice or confetti at weddings. In Athens the bride and bridegroom, as Lear learned with pleasure after *The Owl and the Pussycat* had been written, ate a quince, which was supposed to have the property of promoting fertility.

In Rome a bride's hair, like that of a pregnant high-caste Hindu, was ceremonially parted, for the hair is a favorite haunt of evil spirits. But the Roman used on this occasion a blunted spear-head, called *the bachelor's spear*. Perhaps this custom originated in the remote past when an old disused spear was the handiest iron instrument available in the hut. This strange comb is another example of the magical efficacy of iron. A number of features which could be paralleled in European folklore were attached to the bringing home of the Roman bride. Dressed in new clothes, wearing a veil, and crowned with a wreath, she was formally torn from the arms of her mother and brought to the bridegroom's house by an attendant procession. She was preceded by a boy carrying a torch of white thorn and attended by two other pages, one holding either hand. The fathers and mothers of these three boys

[39]

must all be living, a necessary qualification which is often demanded of performers in other kinds of lucky rituals, e.g. the leader of the *Daphnephoria* procession, a Maypole rite, at Thebes, or the runners in the autumn vintage festival at Athens. At Athens, too, the bride was attended by a boy, both of whose parents were alive, carrying a winnowing basket. The members of the bridal procession sang loud and obscene songs, the noise of which assisted the torch of magical wood in keeping evil at a distance, while the character of the words both averted evil and promoted the fertility of the marriage. We may compare the fertility magic of the obscene dances connected with the Dorian May-wreath (*korythale*), rites which in historical Greece had become associated with Artemis. Meantime the bridegroom scattered nuts for which the young scrambled, a very wide-spread form of fertility charm. Arrived at the new home the bride anointed the door posts with wolves' fat and oil, and wreathed them with wool. Like the bride among the Moslems of South India, she was then lifted and carried in, so that her foot did not touch the threshold.

A modern Persian marriage custom by which

the bridal party passes in procession between the carcasses and severed heads of five sheep, has no counterpart in the wedding ceremonies of Greece and Rome, but it is analogous in purpose and character to the Macedonian and Boeotian practice of purifying an army by marching it between the severed portions of a dog.

A number of primitive beliefs have inevitably left their traces upon the funeral customs of Greece and Rome. A death naturally made the house impure, and a bough was placed at the door to warn passers-by of the fact. In Greece the fire of the household hearth was allowed to go out; it had been contaminated by the infection of death. It was re-lighted with fresh fire only when the ceremonies of purification, which included a thorough sweeping of the house, had been concluded. A vessel of water was placed at the door, so that those who came out of the house of mourning might purify themselves before renewing contact with the world. For the *Superstitious Man* of Theophrastus this precaution was not sufficient. He was so alarmed at the possibility of pollution that he would not pay the last duty of friendship nor enter a dead

[41]

man's house at all. These last visits of friends were paid to the corpse as it lay in state upon a couch, decked with woollen fillets, and crowned with vine leaves, flowers, and magic herbs. Its feet must always be pointed to the door; for it is advisable to indicate to the dead the way out, but not the way back. Some savage peoples go even further. The Tlingit, for example, take a plank from the rear wall of the house and remove the corpse through the hole, for fear that if the door were used, the ghost might return by it. The Moslems of India, amongst other peoples, observe a similar custom.

A curious superstition attached in classical antiquity to persons who had falsely been reported dead in foreign parts. When they returned home, they were not allowed to enter the house by the door. A hole was made in the roof, through which they were lowered, and they were then required to go through a pantomimic ceremony of being treated as a newborn baby. A curiously exact parallel among the Persians will be found in the eighteenth chapter of Morier's *Hajji Baba of Ispahan*. The official " deadness " of such persons made them dangerous to the living, until they had been ceremonially re-born. According to Hesychius, they might never afterwards enter the temple of the Revered Goddesses, perhaps because the powers of the underworld, thanks to the false announcement of their death, had established a certain claim upon them.

At Rome it was the custom for the nearest kinsman of the dying man to inhale his last breath, thereby ensuring the continuity of the family life, in which the lives of individual heads of the family are but successive incidents. Somewhat similarly among the Seminoles of Florida, when a woman died in childbirth, the infant was held over her face to receive her parting spirit.

The belief that children who die in infancy may be re-born to the mother in the persons of later children, is widespread in the Lower Culture. A similar belief is perhaps the explanation of a discovery in settlements belonging to the early Bronze Age in the Aegean. The remains of infants have been found buried in jars underneath the houses, though adults were uniformly buried in cemeteries outside the towns. The explanation of the antique technical term *suggrundaria,* which is given by Fulgentius, suggests that a similar belief was once held by the Romans. In the remote past small children were not cremated but buried under the eaves of the house.

I do not believe that there are any real grounds for thinking that the Greeks and Romans believed in *revenants*, like the Slavonic vampire or animated corpse,[1] from which I personally believe the modern Greek *vrykolakas* to be derived. But the spirits of the dead were popularly supposed to return, though not in this particularly repulsive form, and we may notice a few superstitions with regard to ghosts. It may be well, however, to mention that the popular ideas about ghosts and the underworld were not consistent in antiquity, any more than they are with us, and also that the attitude towards the dead varied considerably at different periods of classical civilization, though in the space at our disposal we cannot attempt to analyze the different stages but must treat classical antiquity as a whole.

The Athenian festival of All Souls was held in the Month of Flowers, Anthesterion, February to March. February in the original Roman calendar was the last month in the year, and as the meaning of its name implies, it was distinguished by ceremonies of purification; the sins of the old year were expiated ere the new year began in March. The family dead, who returned at the *Anthesteria*, do not seem to have been very formidable. The living, it is true, chewed buck-thorn and anointed their house-doors with pitch, for all ghosts, however well disposed, have the taint of death about them, and contact with them is likely to be dangerous. But the ritual seems to have been of a friendly character. On the last of the three days of the festival a pot of porridge was offered in each household to the ancestral dead, and the ceremonies were closed by the head of the house pronouncing the formula: " Be gone, ye ghosts; it is no longer *Anthesteria*." By this the dead were dismissed to their place until the following year.

The Roman festivals for the dead in February (*Parentalia*, Feb. 13–21, and *Caristia*, Feb. 22) seem also to have been rather festivals of commemoration than designed to appease malevolent spirits. The *Lemuria*, however, on the 9th, 11th, and 13th of May, which we have already mentioned in connection with the reluctance to be married in May, had a more sinister aspect. The domestic ceremonies concluded with the following ritual. The householder rises at midnight on the last day of the festival. He has no shoes on his feet, and he makes a gesture of aversion with his hand — the well known ' horn,' which is frequently employed against the evil eye. The thumb is tucked under the two closed middle fingers, and the index and little fingers extended. He washes his hands and takes a number of black beans, which he throws behind him without looking back. As he does this he nine times recites the formula " with these I redeem me and mine." Then he washes his hands again, and brazen vessels, the efficacy of which in driving off evil powers is known throughout the world, are clashed. Then he dismisses the spirits of the dead by the repetition of a charm, again nine times repeated: " Depart, ye *manes* of my fathers." Then at last the rite is at an end, and he may look round.

Turning from these rituals connected with the regular periodic return of the dead upon definite dates, we may notice a few of the popular customs relating to ghosts. Among many peoples, e.g. the Masai, the dead may not be mentioned by name. Strabo noticed this custom among the Albanians, but the Elder Pliny tells us that the Romans themselves, if they had occasion to mention a dead man's name, added a deprecatory formula that they did not wish to disturb his rest. At old Prussian funeral feasts any morsels which fell from the table, were left for the lonely souls who had no relatives to give them food. When the meal was over, the priest swept the souls out of the house, saying: " Dear souls, ye have eaten and drunk." If this formula reminds us of the *Anthesteria,* the leaving of dropped morsels squares with Athenian table manners in the fifth century B.C. What fell from the table must not be picked up, but must be left for the ' heroes,' as ghosts had then come to be called in popular speech. In Persia a meal must not be completely finished; something must be left for the Jinn. In East Prussia to throw rubbish out of the door, might injure the ghosts on the threshold, and readers of the *Arabian Nights* will know how dangerous it is to throw date stones about, when you are lunching by a spring. Probably you will hit an invisible Jinni in the eye and blind him, and then there will be trouble in store for you. In Aristophanes' time to empty a footpan or a bath out of the door was taboo, for fear of injuring the ' heroes.'

By the fifth century B.C. popular superstition in Greece seems to have become more concerned with malevolent ghosts than it had earlier been. 'Heroes' were supposed to 'walk' and might strike the nocturnal wayfarer with paralysis. It was wiser to steal past tombs in silence, for fear of irritating the occupants to emerge and attack you. Such ghosts were black of visage. Pausanias himself saw a copy of the picture of the ghost of Temesa, whom a famous athlete, Euthymus, fought and drove into the sea in order to rescue from him the girl whom he subsequently married. " The ghost was of a horrid black colour, and his whole appearance was most dreadful, and he wore a wolfskin." The classical ghost in general seems either to have appeared as a skeleton or to have been black, not white.

Plato has alluded to the popular belief in

" *those thick and gloomy shadows damp,*
Oft seen in charnel vaults and sepulchres,
Lingering and sitting by a new-made grave
As loth to leave the body that it loved."

Earthy natures, he explains, are held back by their impurities from complete and immediate release from the world of the body. On the other hand another popular superstition, to which Plato also alludes, supposed that the souls of the very wicked were scattered and annihilated in a great wind.

The most dangerous kind of ghost in classical antiquity, as elsewhere, was the spirit of a man who had come by a violent end. The converse of this belief is the supposed efficacy for magical purposes of the remains of such persons. The catalogue of such things in the Elder Pliny shows that the relics of gladiators and executed criminals were as widely used in his time for magical recipes, as were the spoils of the gibbet in England up to the XVIIIth century. A rope or nail from a cross upon which a man had been executed or the hair of the criminal was used, he tells us, as a specific for quartan ague. " This is oftentimes donne in London: " runs Aubrey's comment, " many have great faith in it: yt hangman getts money for pieces of the halters for this purpose."

It is widely believed that the activities of a potentially malevolent ghost may be limited by the mutilation of his body. Thus the Australian natives cut off the right thumb of their dead enemies to prevent their ghosts being able to

hurl a spear. In the Herero War the natives
mutilated the bodies of dead Germans with a
similar motive. Further analogies could be
quoted from the New World. This, no doubt,
was the reason why Athenian suicides, like the
victims of the Scythian human sacrifices in
Herodotus, had their right hands cut off. It
explains too the ghastly practice of *mascha-
lismos*, in accordance with which a murderer
lopped off the hands and feet of his victim and
tied them round the neck of the corpse. This
is what Sophocles makes Clytaemnestra do to
her murdered husband. The motive is to cripple
effectively the activity of the vengeful ghost.

The coin placed in the mouth of a corpse was
said to represent the fare to be paid to Charon,
the infernal ferryman, for his passage across
the Styx. But this is probably an explanatory
story, which is not so old as the rite. Like
" Peter's penny," which was similarly said to
be destined to be given by the dead man to St.
Peter, the money was probably originally
placed with the corpse simply for the use of
the dead man in the next world. When crema-
tion was general, articles intended for the dead
man's use must be burned. Thus in a famous
story of Herodotus, Periander, tyrant of Cor-

inth, sent to an oracle of the dead to ask a question of his wife's ghost. She replied that she was cold for want of clothes and would not answer, until she was properly provided. Periander thereupon stripped the ladies of Corinth of their finery and burned it; his wife was then satisfied and gave him the required information. Similar is the theme of a parody of such stories in Lucian, where the ghost of a dearly loved wife appears to the husband to complain that one of her slippers, which had fallen behind a chest, had been overlooked and had not been burned at her funeral.

Oracles of the dead existed at several places in the classical world; usually they were situated at some natural chasm, often at one which emitted sulphurous exhalations. Such places were supposed to be gateways to the nether regions. Here, as at Endor, the spirits of the dead could be evoked to answer questions. In the later classical antiquity there is also record of the necromancy of Black Magic and the calling back of the unwilling spirit into the corpse by magical conjurations. There were also ventriloquist diviners (the girl exorcised by St. Paul is an example), who were supposed to be possessed by a departed spirit. Something

[51]

similar was the vulgar belief at Rome in possession by *larvae*. Human sacrifice for necromantic purposes was alleged to be practiced in the Black Magic of late classical antiquity. Part of its efficacy depends upon the belief that those about to die are " fey " or prescient. To this superstition, common in Yorkshire and other parts of the British Isles, Plato makes allusion in the *Apology of Socrates*.

The ghost stories of antiquity are not very interesting. They belong to familiar types, e.g. the revelation of the murder in the inn or the story of the philosopher Athenodorus and the apparition in the haunted house which vanished at a spot in the courtyard, beneath which a skeleton in chains was subsequently found. Mr. Collison-Morley, to whose little book on *Greek and Roman Ghost Stories* the curious may be referred, has noted that this latter tale was told in the XVIIIth century in almost identical form as the experience of Gilbert Rule, the founder and first Principal of Edinburgh University. Indeed authentic narratives of apparitions throughout the ages show little originality and make monotonous reading. Little but the names and settings are usually altered.

At the dinner table of the parvenu Trimalchio, in the novel of Petronius, old wives' tales are eagerly recited and swallowed. That tales of wonder were also a feature of after-dinner conversation in more refined circles is shown by the Younger Pliny's letter about the wonderful tame dolphin of Hippo. One of Trimalchio's guests, named Niceros, tells a story of his experiences with a *versipellis* (turn-skin) or werewolf. He set out one night to visit his mistress accompanied by a soldier who was lodging in the same house. What was his horror when, as soon as they reached the tombstones, which, of course, lined the roadsides outside any large town, his companion took off his clothes, put them on the ground and made a ring of water round them! The clothes became stone and the man turned into a wolf. When Niceros reached the house of his mistress, she greeted him with the story of how a large wolf had got in and worried the sheep; it had got away, but one of the slaves had wounded it in the neck with a spear. Sure enough, when Niceros on his return came to the place where the clothes had been, he found only a pool of blood and when he reached his lodging the soldier was in bed with a sore neck. We are reminded of how old women suspected of being witches have been found with identical injuries to those which had been inflicted on a cat or a hare.

Classical witches had the usual tastes of such creatures for graveyards, where they could be found at midnight muttering their spells and collecting their noxious herbs. They were reputed to be able to draw down the moon by spells. The most famous witches, in accordance with a very general psychology, were thought to be those of backward or remote districts. The Marsians in the time of Ennius were popularly renowned for wizardry, and the Sabellian witches were notorious in the days of Horace. But the home of classical witchcraft was Thessaly, where the earlier scenes of Apuleius' novel are laid. This work contains some admirable witch stories. We may notice in particular the tale of how the witches cut the throat of their victim, extracted his heart, and closed the wound with a sponge. The unfortunate man wakes up apparently well and sound, but as soon as he reaches running water he is seized with thirst, the sponge drops out, and he falls down dead. A belief in this form of magical murder in which the victim is apparently uninjured but has really had his internal organs removed by a magician or witch, is widely distributed. Thus for example the Cherokee " Spear-finger " takes his victims' livers. They go about their affairs to all appearances uninjured, but they gradually pine away and eventually die. In India among the Santal Parganas witches eat the victims' liver without any wound appearing; the man dies in a few days. Further parallels might be quoted from New Guinea and elsewhere.

To turn from witches to less noxious supernatural beings, everyone who has read Irish fairy tales, knows that the Cluricaune is a little fellow " with a little bit of an apron on him, and a hammer in his hand, and a little red night-cap on his head and he is making a shoe." If you succeed in catching him, while he is intent on his shoe-making, you can make him give you his magic purse which always has a shilling in it, however much you spend. One of the diners at Trimalchio's table alludes to a similar Roman belief, when he supposes that a man who has suddenly and inexplicably risen from indigence to affluence, must have succeeded in seizing a goblin's (*incubo*) hat and so acquired his treasure. Again a mention of ' fairy gold,' of the kind which turns to ashes on the morrow, to which there is allusion in proverbial usage, will be found in Lucian's account of the misanthrope Timon of Athens. With the dwarfs of Europe we may perhaps compare the rather shadowy figures of the Idaean Dactyls, magical inventors of metallurgy, who were but a finger high. The stupid ogress, the Lamia who eats little children and keeps her eyes in a box, the Acco and Gello whose stupidity was as remarkable as that of the *dhrakos'* wife in modern Greek stories, were also known to antiquity.

Many similar superstitions with regard to the world of nature are to be found in ancient and in modern folklore. In Greece a local reverence was paid to certain birds and animals, which was once regarded as evidence of a hypothetical period of totemism through which the Greeks had passed. The totemic stage of Greek culture, however, has become more hypothetical, the more closely the Greek evidence and the facts about totemism elsewhere have been examined. In Thessaly storks were revered because they killed snakes, and to injure one was regarded as a crime. In the island of Seriphos, for what reason we do not know, lobsters were regarded with superstitious reverence. Aristophanes mentions the custom of saluting the first kite seen in the year, with which we might compare taking off your hat to a magpie. Fishermen sacrificed to Poseidon the first tunny of the catch. The first fish caught is very frequently the subject of special treatment. Sometimes, like the Scottish " king of herring," it must be put back; or like the first fish on West African rivers, it must be talked to " with a sweet mouth."

Hesiod, whose poems reflect the life on a Greek farm in the eighth century B.C., has special names for animals. The snail, for example, he calls " the house-carrier "; in parts of rural England it is called " the hodmandod." In some cases such expressions may be euphemistic, as when Hesiod warns us not to let a boy sit upon " the things which must not be moved," i.e. tombstones. It would be as unlucky to say "tombstones" as to say "fairies" instead of " the little people." But often these periphrases may be due simply to the attraction which verbal quibbles have for simple minds. Bompas notices this trait in the Santal Parganas, who will, for instance, call " a mother " " a milk tree," just as Hesiod calls a hand " the thing with five branches." This rather childish taste for verbal ingenuity may under certain conditions be elaborated into a conventional poetic diction like that of the Scandinavian *skalds* with their " battle dew " for blood, or " ship's road " for sea, or " flame of the sea " for gold. But perhaps we may look nearer home and consider the peculiar jargon in which a cricket or baseball match is habitually reported in our newspapers.

The early farmer dated his seasonal operations largely by the habits of animals and birds, and he used them as weather prophets. ' Just-so stories,' aetiological legends is their more formidable technical name, were invented to account for their peculiarities of appearance or habit. To give one instance, the cry of the woodpecker in Eastern Europe is popularly supposed to bring rain, and he is called the *giessvogel*. The story is told that once God ordered the beasts to dig a well; the *giessvogel* said that he was afraid of dirtying his fine clothes. In consequence he was cursed that he should drink out of no pond. Hence in dry weather he cries " *giet* " for rain to quench his parching thirst. In the analogous Greek story, Apollo sent the raven to fetch water. The bird dallied on the way to wait for some corn to get ripe in order to eat it, and so forgot his orders That is why he is punished with perpetual thirst and croaks hoarsely for rain. In Tyrol a story is told how the raven prevented the Holy Child from drinking, with similar results.

The lugubrious or weird character of certain animal cries has everywhere earned them a sinister significance. The Greeks were not alone in regarding as evil omens the cawing of a crow, the hooting of an owl, or the howling of a dog. For a weasel to cross your path is regarded as unlucky in the north of England, as it was in Athens by the *Superstitious Man*. Both the modern and the ancient farmer beat brass pans when the bees swarm. With us to call a boy ' a cuckoo ' or ' a gowk ' is not to flatter his intelligence. The comic poet Plato made his Meleager " go about everywhere like a stupid cuckoo." Dogs, again, are almost everywhere credited with the power of being able to see spirits, which are invisible to the mortal eye. In Greece the belief was as old as Homer, who describes the dogs cowering at the invisible presence of the goddess in the palace at Ithaca. The observation that dogs lick their injuries has very generally attributed medicinal virtue to the dog's tongue. At Epidaurus there is record of an Aeginetan boy whose tumours were cured by the licking of dogs, and Sextus Empiricus mentions the use of dogs' flesh as medicine. In 1884 it was believed in the Punjab that the English killed dogs for the *amrita* in their tongues.

The charms and magical formulas for dealing with agricultural pests are innumerable. Pliny recommends putting up the skulls of horses as a charm in gardens. I have myself seen them so used in modern Crete. Against caterpillars Columella directs that a young menstruous girl should walk three times round the garden with bare feet and loosened hair and garments. The bare feet, the circle, the number three, and the efficacy of menstrual blood are all commonplaces of magical ritual. Here is another spell against mice, in which placation is pleasantly tempered with warning. " I adjure you, ye mice here present, that ye neither injure me nor suffer another mouse to do so. I give you yonder field (compare the Scottish farmers' practice of marking off an area for the powers of evil, *the Guid Man's Croft*), but if ever I catch you here again, by the Mother of the Gods, I will rend you in seven pieces."

In more than one Greek cult the god has been given a title from the vermin which he averts [e.g. Apollo Parnopios (Locust)], and it is possible that Apollo Smintheus (Field Mouse), who was worshipped in Rhodes and in the Troad, was originally a vermin god. What is rather curious about this latter cult is a story the distribution of which needs investigation. In Egypt Herodotus heard how the mice came to the rescue of the country and gnawed the bowstrings of Sennacherib's men, thereby frustrating his invasion. An identical story was told in connection with the foundation of the cult of Apollo Smintheus in the Troad. But more remarkable still, it turns up again in Khotan! In all three cases the tale serves to explain the meaning of a statue of a god or king with a mouse in his hand or at his feet.

An appendix to the agricultural poem of Hesiod contains a large number of rules of avoidance, lucky and unlucky days, and things you must not do. For example, nails must not be cut upon a religious festival, with which we may compare Pliny's rule that the last day

of the Roman secular week should be avoided
for this purpose or the modern superstition that
it is unlucky to trim the nails on Sunday. Many
of these primitive taboos prescribed by Hesiod
were taken up by the Pythagoreans and were
given mystical meanings by them. Among the
Pythagorean rules was the avoidance of beans,
which were taboo also to the *Flamen Dialis*.
Into the various interpretations ancient and
modern of the significance of the bean it would
take too long to go, but the ' lucky bean ' is
still to be seen on sale in the cheaper jewelry
stores. Pliny recommends you to take a bean
with you for luck when you go to auctions.

The minor superstitions of every day are
singularly constant. Lucky days did not go out
with Hesiod, nor even with Trimalchio, upon
whose calendar they were specially marked.
Almost any magazine will offer you an anti-
rheumatic ring. One of Aristophanes' worthies
possessed a magic ring, and a character of
Antiphanes wore one against indigestion. In
antiquity too they were pretty cheap; each of
these cost only a drachma apiece. The waxing
and the waning of the moon are still a matter
of concern to some. Varro tells us to cut corn
with a waxing moon, but to fell timber, shear

sheep, cut our hair (unless we want to go bald) with a waning moon. Pliny prescribes the 16th or 28th days of the moon for hair-cutting in order to avoid baldness and headache. From Petronius we learn that cutting hair or nails at sea was thought to raise a storm. As among many savage peoples the cuttings were often carefully preserved, for fear that someone might use them for magical purposes against you. Trimalchio kept his beard trimmings in a golden box. Special precautions were taken over the disposal of the hair trimmings of the *Flamen Dialis* or those of the Vestal Virgins. To prevent galling between the legs Pliny recommends a sprig of mint, and persons going a long way on foot are advised to carry a myrtle stick. Aubrey tells us that the Wiltshire farmers and graziers used to carry a piece of elder stick in their pockets to preserve them from galling.

It is probably the practice in most nurseries, when boiled eggs have been eaten, to invert the shell and break in the top, lest the fairies or witches should use them. " There is no one," says Pliny, " who does not dread being spellbound by means of evil imprecations; and hence the practice, after eating eggs or snails, of immediately breaking the shells or piercing them with the spoon."

Lucky and unlucky signs are still observed. Odd numbers are still counted lucky by gamblers, as they were by Virgil and Pliny; English farmers' wives, like the Romans, set for choice an odd number of eggs beneath the hen. For omens, Tiberius Gracchus stumbled on the doorstep on the day of his death; Augustus became anxious if inadvertently he tried while dressing " to cram a right hand foot into a left hand shoe." Trimalchio kept a special slave at the door to remind each guest as he arrived to enter " with the right foot first." The Greeks and Romans wished their friends who sneezed good health, as we say " Gesundheit " and " God bless you." Like Pliny, we still wish our friends " a Happy New Year " on January 1st for luck. " Why," asks Aristotle, " are sneezes unlucky between midnight and midday, but lucky between midday and midnight? " Of the unlucky morning sneeze Reginald Scot records that " many will go to bed againe if they sneeze before their shoes be on their feet."

Augustus' dreams were least reliable in spring, and ancient superstition agreed with modern that morning dreams were surest of fulfilment. The Berbers of North Africa agree about the morning dream, but prefer the spring among the seasons. When the *Superstitious Man* has had a dream, " he will go to the interpreter of dreams, the seers, the augurs, to ask them to what god or goddess he ought to pray." In Plautus, dreams are averted by religious ritual; in Greek tragedy relief is found by telling them to the open sky. Among Moslems of North Africa after a bad dream spit on the right and say " I take refuge with God " and never tell it to anyone. The Turkish traveller Evliya " did away the evil of the night " by almsgiving.

Most of the minor methods of divination were practised in antiquity. The sieve and shears were consulted by the peasants of Theocritus; the method of the Bible and key or the Moslem practice of acquiring responses from the chance opening of the Koran or the works of Sadi or Hafiz were preceded by the *sortes Homericae* and the *sortes Vergilianae.* The latter were in use as early as Hadrian, and were employed throughout the Middle Ages. A famous historical example of their use is the warning of his fate, which Charles I elicited from the copy of Virgil which is now in Bodley's Library at Oxford. Kledonism, or the drawing of omens from the overhearing of chance utterances, was practised in ancient, as it is in modern Greece and in other parts of Europe. Divination by the pendulum, which is very commonly worked with a ring and a human hair as a nursery game today, was known to antiquity. "May I never have any dealings," said Plato, "with the diviners, as they are called, who in any way or manner counsel me to take up the deposit entrusted to the earth." The methods of divination for buried treasure were not, however, those of Dousterswivel, for there is no evidence of the use of the "dowser's rod" by the Greeks and Romans. The love charms of Simaetha in Theocritus or the waxen image, which is pricked by needles, as described by Ovid, are among the commonplaces of European popular magic. Crystal-gazing in oil poured into the hollow of a shield is mentioned by Aristophanes, and the magical mirror well, which reflects distant scenes and events on its surface, was known to Pausanias.

A conspectus of ancient folklore drawn up upon the plan of the Folklore Society's volumes of *County Folklore,* would include sections upon natural objects, local shrines, seasonal festivals, games, songs, riddles, and proverbs. These sections it would be easy enough to fill up for the ancient world, did space permit. The first would include curious natural rocks, to which legends had become attached, like the famous weeping figure of Niobe upon Mt. Sipylus, the petrified ship of the Phaeacians at Corcyra or Polydectes and the wicked islanders at Seriphos. Then we should have a list of wells or springs to which a magical origin was attached, like those which were caused by the hoof of Pegasus, the club of Heracles, Atalanta's spear, or Poseidon's trident. Next would come waters which possessed magical properties, e.g., which petrify objects thrown into them or colour the wool of the local sheep or heal specific diseases. Into healing springs coins of gold and silver were often cast, as they are into the local healing wells of rustic England. For local shrines there would be rich material in the cults of heroes, persons legendary or historical, who were supposed once to have lived on earth as human beings, but to have been canonized after death. The features of their cult could be exactly paralleled from the local cults of Christian and Moslem saints.

Divination and healing were particularly prominent in the folklore aspects of their worship, and in Greece, as elsewhere, incubation, i.e., the practice of making the enquirer or the patient sleep at the shrine, was the most usual method of obtaining responses or regaining health.

For seasonal festivals we should be called upon to notice such practices as rain-making by spilling water from a large jar taken round in procession on a cart (Crannon in Thessaly), or the ritual sprinkling of water with a bough dipped in a sacred spring by the priest in times of drought (Mt. Lykaion in Arcadia). The Roman Catholic Rogation ritual and our " beating of the bounds " are almost certainly a direct inheritance from the ancient Roman *Ambarvalia* or annual lustration of the fields. The " need fires " find their parallel in the ceremonies of the Roman *Parilia,* when the herds were driven through the magical flames and their shepherds leaped over the bonfires. The evidence about analogous fire-festivals in Greece has been discussed by Professor Nilsson in the forty-second volume of the *Journal of Hellenic Studies.* The concluding ceremony of the Roman agricultural year on October 15, with its races, the sacrifice of the near horse of the winning pair (called *the October Horse*), the preservation of its blood for fertility medicine, and the subsequent fight between the inhabitants of two of the wards of Rome for the possession of its head, has many counterparts in European folklore.

Then there is the scape-goat ritual of the Ionian *Thargelia,* in which the ills of the community were annually loaded on to two criminals. They were beaten with purifying and fructifying plants (an inconsistent killing of two birds with one stone is not an infrequent phenomenon in folklore), and originally they were slain, their bodies burned upon the wood of unfruitful trees, and their ashes scattered to the winds. Such festivals again as the Greek *Cronia* or the Roman *Saturnalia,* in which masters waited upon slaves, and there was a general licensed equality of merrymaking and a mutual interchange of presents among friends, have obvious modern parallels. In festivals of this character, it was sometimes the custom for the men to dress up as women and the women as men, like the ' guise dancing' of Devon and Cornwall. The assumption of the clothes of the opposite sex was also a feature of some local marriage customs in Greece. This too can be paralleled from observances elsewhere, and the motive is probably to cheat by disguise the evil eye or other magical malevolence.

A number of examples of May-pole ceremonies, the *Daphnephoria* at Thebes, the *Eiresione* customs at Athens, the obscene dances connected with the Dorian May-wreath (*korythale*), I have collected in *Folklore Studies Ancient and Modern*. There too I have quoted a number of children's songs and singing games. They include those of the house-to-house collecting variety, like the Crow Song or the Swallow Song of Rhodes, with which our Hunting of the Wren may be compared; nursery jingles, like " Come out, dear sun," the counterpart to our " Rain, rain, go to Spain " ; counting-out games, like Torty Tortoise or what is obviously akin to " Here we come gathering nuts in May,"

Where are my roses, where are my violets, where is my beautiful parsley?
These are my roses, these are my violets, and this is my beautiful parsley.

Games similar to the majority of those which are played in our streets or nurseries, can be found in existence in antiquity, for instance Prisoners' Base, Blind Man's Buff, Ducks and Drakes, Hie-spy, or Chuckies. For work songs, there is the famous mill song of Lesbos:

> Grind, *mill, grind,*
> For *Pittacus too grinds,*
> Who *is king in great Mitylene.*

Riddles, the taste for which is universal, are everywhere pretty similar. The famous riddle of the Sphinx, which it took an Oedipus to solve, is current, in substance the same, among the Mongols and among the peasants of Gascony. In the Greek form it ran: " What is that which on earth is two-footed, three-footed, and four-footed, and is weakest when it has most feet?" The answer, of course, is man, who crawls as an infant and supports the tottering steps of age with a staff. Another favourite was the eunuch and the bat:

A *man, but not a man, but still a man (i.e. an eunuch),*
Casting *a stone but not a stone (a pumice stone) destroyed,*
A *bird, but not a bird, but still a bird (a bat),*
Perched *on a stick, but not a stick (a reed).*

Popular gnomic wisdom, again, does not differ very much in different countries or ages. Hence it is not surprising to find that the famous *skolion* (drinking catch) of Simonides

To *have health is best for mortal man,*
Se*cond best to be of beautiful form,*
T*hird to be rich without fraud,*
An*d fourth to be in the prime of youth with his friends around him*

has close parallels in modern Greek folksong, the *Avesta*, and the *Edda*.[2] Proverbs, too, need not perhaps detain us. Their detailed discussion would take too long, while their generic similarities are too patent to require it. "One swallow does not make the summer," for example, which Aristotle knew as a proverbial saying, has its equivalent in many languages. The mice, which in Cicero's time deserted a house about to fall, are equivalent to the rats which still desert a sinking ship. But we may notice one example of a proverb which cannot, I think, have occurred spontaneously in more than one area. The phrase "where the mice eat iron" for "nowhere in the world," or alternatively for a poor country destitute of resources, is as old as Herodas in classical usage, but the droll

[72]

from which the expression seems to be derived, occurs frequently and early in Indian literature.[3] Had it been unknown to the Greeks, its European distribution might have been attributed to the medieval popularity of *Kalila and Dimna* or works founded upon the *Panchatantra* and other Indian story-books. But Seneca and Herodas cannot have got it from *Kalila and Dimna*. The proverb, in fact, raises in an acute form the problem of the relation of classical to oriental *Märchen* and fables, which will mainly occupy us in the next chapter.

III. FOLKTALES·AND FABLES

MYTH, legend, and folktale it is convenient to distinguish. Myths are explanatory stories, which have been invented to explain how the world and the things in it came to be, or to describe and so to define the nature and peculiarities of the divine powers, or to give a reason for some ritual custom, the origin of which has really been lost with the lapse of time. It is obvious that myths about gods or about ritual are bound up with the particular conception of divine beings whose nature they seek to illustrate or explain, and with the particular customs for which they attempt to account. We are not likely here to find stories of universal distribution, except in so far as material has been borrowed from folktale and adapted to the particular purpose of myth. With regard to cosmogonic myths the case is rather different. Here the same problems (e.g., how did the world come into existence or how did the practice of the arts which distinguish man from animals take their origin?) everywhere propound them-

selves to man, and certain similarly simple answers are likely to suggest themselves to him
independently in many parts of the world.
Thus to the first question that the marriage of
sky and earth was the prelude to the birth of
things is the solution which is offered in widely
separate countries, and to the second that some
great culture hero learned or stole from the
gods the secrets which had earlier been a divine
monopoly, and had conferred the knowledge
upon man, is an answer which has independently suggested itself to many peoples. Very
often, as in the case of the Greek Prometheus,
who stole fire in a reed and gave it to man, such
activities on behalf of mankind at the expense
of divine prerogatives have been supposed to
have caused an enmity between the gods and
the benefactor of human civilization.

Such general answers to universal problems
inevitably occur to human beings everywhere
as soon as they begin to reflect upon their own
existence. It is, therefore, not surprising to find
that the marriage of the Sky and the Earth and
their subsequent forcible separation occurs in
Maori mythology as well as in Greek, or that
the story is also told in the Antipodes of how
evil came into the world through the curiosity

of a woman. In Greece, it will be remembered, Pandora had been entrusted with a box with strict injunctions not to look inside it; feminine curiosity prevailed, she opened it, and thus let loose all the ills of life which had been securely shut up within it. There is, however, no need here to attempt the formidable task of tracing links of transmission between Greece and New Zealand; for such relatively simple and obvious ideas are probably due to independent invention. Coincidence, again, is usually the true explanation of the similarity in the stories which are told to explain the peculiar cries or habits of animals, like the stories of the *giessvogel* and the raven, which have been mentioned above. The problem set is more or less the same in different countries, e.g., why a particular bird has a crest of gold (the king wren) or why its cry seems to portend rain; it is almost inevitable that the same kind of stories should be invented to account for them. Again the Greeks said that games had been invented in Lydia in time of famine in order that the distraction might mitigate the pangs of hunger, and that Palamedes had invented draughts and dice to make tolerable the hungry monotony of the Greek fleet, when weather-bound and short of

supplies. In the East chess was said to have
been invented during the siege of the capital
of Ceylon by Rama, to allay the anxiety of
Mandodari, Ravana's wife, the pieces moving
on the board to represent the greater contest
taking place outside the walls. There is a generic resemblance between all these tales, but
they are all the kind of inventions which might
naturally suggest themselves to anyone who was
called upon to elucidate the problem, " How did
games ever come to be played? "

Legend, our second category, is popular history. Its distinguishing characteristic is that it
contains an element of historical fact for its
core. Round the historical nucleus mythical and
folktale elements have collected and to a
greater or lesser degree have obscured for us
the accuracy of the information which it contains. But in so far as it is legend, it is connected with a specific country and with particular, if dimly remembered, persons or events.
The historian's difficulty in handling it is that,
though he is well aware that there is in tradition a substratum of truth, unless there exists
some external and independent evidence to act
as a touchstone, there is often no means of de-
ciding what part of it is true and what is fiction.

The term folktale we apply to stories which are told primarily for amusement, sometimes for edification combined with amusement, e.g., fables. They are a kind of elementary novel. Both myth and legends often borrow and employ elements which properly belong to folktale, but in themselves they differ from folktale, because they have a purpose either explanatory or historical. Although from time to time far-fetched attempts have been made to find solar mythology in *Little Red Riding Hood* or esoteric meanings, which are alleged to be concealed beneath an elaborate system of allegory, in the other favourites of the nursery, such ingenuities are a waste of time and show a lack of common sense. The obvious object of folktales, drolls, and fables is to entertain the audience to whom they are told.

Now the impetus given to the study of these popular stories by the work of the Brothers Grimm in the early part of the last century has resulted in the accumulation of a large amount of material from all parts of the world. From these collections it has become evident that there is an Indo-European group of stories; that is to say any one collection of folktales from any country lying between Iceland and

[78]

India will be found to contain a large proportion of stories in common with any other collection from another country within the same broad area.

The first question which arises is whether this similarity is to be accounted for by independent invention or by transmission. Obviously our answer will depend in part upon our definition of similarity. If, by similarity we mean but a general vague analogy in idea, clearly it will be unnecessary to postulate transmission. This needs to be emphasized, for it is often forgotten in the eager pastime of spinning theories. Suppose we were examining the modern novel and attempted to work with some such general and vague formula as this. "A lack of sympathy between a married couple and the pity aroused in a hero or heroine by the unhappiness of the more sensitive member of the unfortunate union, causes him or her to fall in love with his or her affinity. The accidental death of the unsympathetic husband or wife eventually enables the lovers to marry." Common sense would surely forbid us to suppose either that all novels which could be reduced to this simple scheme were in fact identical, or that this simple formula which is rooted in the psychology of human beings and the practical difficulties arising from the conditions of civilized marriage, must necessarily have been the exclusive invention of one particular genius, which all the other authors have plagiarized. The same common sense should be applied to the classification of folktales. It should forbid us, on the one hand, to seek for a single origin of a simple formula, which may well have occurred independently to more than one storyteller, e.g., such a formula as " a hero wins the hand of a princess by the performance of magical tasks." On the other hand it suggests the futility of treating, let us say, the story of *Jason and Medea*, as substantially identical with every other story to which this very vague and simple formula can be applied.

Only stories which substantially repeat the same plot, that is to say the same series of incidents arranged in the same logical order of interest, in which the variation is limited to obvious or accidental omissions or modifications, can fairly be treated as variants of the same tale. But where similarity of this kind does exist, it is very difficult to suppose that coincidence and independent invention can account for the occurrence of the variants in different countries. The classic example is the tale of how the hero sets out to recover a stolen talisman with the help of a faithful dog and cat. The villain has secreted the talisman in his mouth, but the cat catches a mouse and terrorizes it into putting its tail up the villain's nose, while he is asleep. As a result the villain coughs or sneezes, out drops the talisman and is picked up by the dog. On the way back, while swimming across some water, a dispute arises between the animals, and the dog, opening his mouth to argue with the cat, drops the talisman into the water, whence, however, it is eventually recovered by a fish. Now to attribute the recurrence of a chain of incidents like this in a number of different areas to independent invention is plainly to ask too much of coincidence. This elaborate series can only have been invented once, and I have no doubt that Cosquin was right in this particular instance in tracing the origin of the story to India.

Genuine identity of plot, therefore, must presuppose that a story was invented once and for all in some one place and has passed elsewhere by transmission. Some scholars have gone further and have attempted to discover a single source from which all European folktales are derived. India they regard as this original home of the fairy tale.[4] With this extreme view I do not personally agree. I should be inclined to criticize the interpretation of the evidence upon which it is based, and it seems to me inherently improbable. But for our immediate purposes, which hardly allow of elaborate discussion, I must content myself with indicating very briefly my own view as to the probable history of European folktales.

The individual folktales I myself believe to have originated in a number of different areas, and I should suspect that folktale transmission has normally been by exchange. There are indeed certain types, e.g., the *Bluebeard* group of tales or *Polyphemus*, the distribution and peculiarities of the variants of which seem to me to indicate that they have travelled eastwards from the west. On the other hand it is true that the form in which the larger proportion of modern European folktales are extant today, is probably to be derived from Eastern originals. The reason for this predominance I should explain by the fact that professional storytelling early became an important art in the East and that collections of such stories were made into books. The result was that when these stories

arrived in Europe, they had a more definite
and permanent form, were in fact technically
better stories, than those which had remained
current upon the basis of oral tradition, which
invariably leads to a disintegration of structure
and failure of precision. Whatever may be
true of money, good stories will always drive
out bad.

As we shall see later, there are difficult instances of correspondence between Eastern and
Western stories which go back as early as the
fifth century B.C., but it was in the Middle
Ages that the great influx of oriental stories
took place. Under the Abbaside caliphs the
great Indian collections of stories were translated and thus passed into Persian and Arabic
literature. The pilgrimages to Jerusalem and the
Levant trade played their part in transmitting
them further westward, but it was mainly in
the period of the Crusades that oriental stories
may be said to have flooded Europe. Hagiology
had earlier been affected, as for example in the
famous *History of St. Barlaam and St. Josa-
phat,* attributed to St. John of Damascus, the
material of which is mainly derived from
Buddhist sources. In medieval Europe books
like the *History of the Seven Wise Men,* a

translation of an oriental collection of tales, in its various forms and editions became widely popular as a source of secular entertainment. A very potent influence too in the distribution of eastern stories among the people was the medieval practice of employing them to add amusement to, or to point the edification of, popular sermons. There exists a whole series of collections of such *exempla,* as they were called, which served as practical handbooks for parsons. Such were the *Disciplina Clericalis* of Alphonsus, the *Exempla* of Jacques de Vitry, the *Gesta Romanorum* or, latest in date, the *Schimpf und Ernst* of Johannes Pauli. Again the writers of *fabliaux* of the XIVth and XVth centuries made use of similar material for purposes of popular satire;[5] later the writers of *novelle,* Straparola and Basile, Sachetti and Boccaccio draw upon the same source for plots to be presented or worked up. The gulf between the *novelle* and the modern collections by folklorists is bridged by the Arcadian interests of the XVIIIth century as represented by Perrault and La Fontaine, or perhaps more characteristically by the Comtesse d'Aulnoy and the *Cabinet des Fées.*

There was, that is to say, a continuous literary tradition reinforcing the oral tradition, an important point, for the effect of literature upon folktale is considerable, though it is often underrated. I have elsewhere quoted instances in which a popular tradition can be shown to be derived directly from a written source, and will here confine myself to one example. In modern Crete a story is told of a plant called κελπέρη, which confers magical vision. Now *kelperi* is not a Greek word, but it is a metathesized form of the German *kerpel* or chervil. The identical story was popular in the medieval German *fabliaux* and in them the plant is called *kerpel*. It surely must follow that, through whatever channel it may have passed, the Cretan story must have its ultimate origin in the German *fabliau*.[6]

It is perhaps remarkable that constant as has been its influence upon the sophisticated literature of Europe, the higher classical mythology and literature has exercised very little direct influence upon folktale. I have somewhere read a distorted version of *Orpheus and Eurydice* told by an American negro, which no doubt has arisen from some classically minded white man entertaining a coloured audience. But if we put aside cases like this, there are very few instances known to me of popular stories which are derived directly from classical literature. There is one, however, which is curious in itself and has a curious distribution. In several parts of modern Greece a story is told to account for the position of the chapels of St. Elias upon the tops of mountains. St. Elias was a sailor who got so tired of the sea, that he shouldered his oar and went off until he could find a village where they were so ignorant of the sea that they did not know what an oar was. At last on the top of the mountain when he asked them what the oar was, they said " a bit of stick "; so there he stuck his oar upright, built a hut, and settled down. The same motif occurs in a sailor's saying, which is current in the British navy today and has been traced back as early as 1871. Nowhere else in modern folklore, so far as I can learn, does it occur. That both are ultimately derived from the *Odyssey* can hardly be doubted. Odysseus, it will be remembered, was told to put his oar on his shoulder and travel until he came to a land where, so ignorant are the natives of the sea, that a wayfarer will mistake his oar for a winnowing shovel. There he is to plant his oar upright in the ground and offer sacrifices to Poseidon.

Speaking generally, there are some instances, as we shall see, where stories told by the ancient Greeks and Romans are identical in plot with modern folktales, but there are not very many, indeed far fewer than is usually supposed, if, as I have suggested, we are rigourous in demanding a real correspondence of plot. On the other hand single incidents or general ideas, which recur in European folktales, are common enough, but with regard to such correspondences a large allowance must be made for coincidence.

This state of affairs is what we should naturally expect to find, if we are right in thinking that the majority of the forms of European folktales are due to the importation of oriental stories in the Middle Ages. But another factor must also be taken into consideration. Our classical material is not derived from any designed collection of the stories which were told for amusement by the common folk in antiquity. The only complete folktale, which is recited as such, so far as I can remember, is the story of *Cupid and Psyche,* which is told by the old woman in the robber's cave in the novel of Apuleius. Our folktale material really consists of the folktale elements, which have been adapted to the special purposes of mythology and legend. It represents therefore fragments in a new and special setting, fragments, moreover, which have been worked up. Here we may particularly notice the strong rationalizing tendency of the Greek mind, and with Professor Nilsson may perhaps suppose that the more barbaric or magical features have often been mitigated or suppressed.

Leaving fables and drolls aside for the moment, let us then consider some examples of the kind of correspondences which occur between classical mythology and Indo-European folktales. Once more our treatment cannot, of course, be exhaustive; it can only illustrate the kinds of correspondences which exist.

Now as regards both general ideas and isolated incidents, there is a quite considerable degree of correspondence. But the resemblances of general ideas, as we have seen, are too vague to help us much in classification. With regard to single incidents the probabilities of independent invention or transmission would seem to me to vary with the character and distribu-

tion of each particular incident. But I must
confess that I can suggest no touchstone of dis-
crimination except the scientifically unsatisfac-
tory one of subjective impression. It may be
well, however, to note that most of the isolated
incidents occur in classical mythology in a different series or setting, to that in which they
normally occur in European folktale.

Jason's companions on the Argonaut include
Heracles the strong man, Polydeukes the boxer,
the sons of Boreas who fly like the wind,
Lynkeus of the keen sight, and so on. Similar
magically endowed champions appear at the
court of King Arthur in the *Red Book of Her-
gest*. But there is no reason to suppose any connection between the *Tale of Kilwych and
Olwen* and the *Saga of the Argonauts* upon
that account, nor is either in any true sense
a variant of any of the group of folktales about
the Champions of which Grimm No. 71 represents one type. The story of the archer Alcon,
who shot the snake which encircled his son
with such dexterity that the arrow did not
penetrate through the snake's body to injure
the child, has no relation to the Teutonic and
Scandinavian tale of the *Wilhelm Tell* type.

Iphiclus could run over corn without bend-

ing it and over the sea without sinking, a fleetness also possessed by the horses, sired by the
North Wind, of Milesian Ericthonius and by
those which Idas or Pelops received from
Poseidon. Obviously this is a folktale motif,
but it is the kind of idea appropriate to the
genre, which might occur independently many
times over.

The idea of marriage tests to win a bride occurs everywhere in folktales, but is too general
to give us any help in classification. In Greece,
partly perhaps because of the rationalistic bent
of the Greek mind and partly because of the
special interest of the Greeks in athletic con-
tests, this episode tends to take the form of
racing. Hippodamia is to be won by the man
who beats her father in the chariot race; races
are set for the suitors of Penelope, Pallene, and
the Danaids; the story of Atalanta gives us yet
another form. Iole is to be given to the suitor
who can beat her father Eurytus in shooting
with the bow. But magical tests also occur.
Apart from the familiar story of Jason, Ad-
metus wins Alcestis by performing, with Apollo's help, the task of yoking a lion and a boar.

The external soul we find in the story of
Meleager, whose mother, angered by his slay-

ing of her brothers, burned the fatal brand upon which his life depended. The brand is absent from the oldest, the Homeric, version of the story, which contains, however, *The Neglected Fairy* motif; for the trouble had arisen through the forgetfulness of Meleager's father, Oineus, who omitted to summon Artemis with the other gods and goddesses to his harvest-home. The child who is suckled by a bear (e.g. Paris) or the winning of a fairy bride (e.g. Peleus and Thetis) are general themes which occur everywhere in folktales, but may have occurred independently in different areas. The circumstances of the winning of Thetis may perhaps be paralleled by the popular ballads of *The Twa Magicians* type, though it would be hardy to maintain that the ballad necessarily derived from the classical myth. It may be noted in passing that the widely distributed *Swan Maiden* motif does not occur, so far as I am aware, in classical folklore.

Mr. Hartland has written an exceedingly valuable and learned work in three volumes to show that *The Legend of Perseus* is the parent of Grimm No. 60. But in fact his theory demands the reconstruction of a hypothetical older form of the classical story, for the existence of

which there is no other reason. Nor does it even
so correspond exactly. I should agree with
Bolte and Polívka that he has failed in his
main purpose. Once more the resemblances
with which we have actually to deal are of a
vague and general order. The idea of the de-
struction of a dragon, which defends a spring,
is to be seen in its simplest form in the fights
between Apollo and the Python or Cadmus and
the Snake. Of the winning of a bride by rescu-
ing her from a monster, *St. George and the
Dragon,* a number of forms occur in Greek
mythology and legend — Perseus and Andro-
meda, Heracles and Hesione, or the legends of
Cleostratus of Thespiae, Eurybatus of Delphi,
and, perhaps we might include, Euthymus and
the Ghost (p. 48 above).

More distinctive, it seems to me, is the use
by Perseus of the cap of darkness, the shoes of
swiftness, and the magical wallet.[7] The acquisition by the hero of similar magical objects is
widely distributed, but the mode of acquisition
tends to fall into two types, acquisition by gift
from some friendly magical person or acquisition by fraud practised upon the previous pos-
sessors. On the whole the first is more general
in the West and the second in the East. The

interesting thing about the story of Perseus is
that there is evidence of the early existence in
Greece of two different versions representing
these alternative methods of acquisition respectively. Further the *kibisis,* as the wallet is
called, is not a Greek word; possibly it is Ana-
tolian. Whether the *kibisis* was originally a
tischen-deck-dich, which has been adapted to
the particular purpose of the Gorgon story, I
am not sure. But it is not impossible. If so, it is
the only exact counterpart of the magic table of
Grimm's stories in classical antiquity, though
Amalthea's horn and Fortunatus' purse have
a certain generic resemblance. The apparent
tischen-deck-dich in the comic poet Crates is
really deceptive. It is a chance coincidence in
a parody of the alleged delightful ease of the
Golden Age. The whole passage indeed is nearer
akin to the *lügenmärchen* of *Schlauraffenland*
(Grimm 158), though it has not any direct
literary connection with it.

The flight of Jason and Medea was regarded
by Andrew Lang as a variant of Grimm 79, in
which a pair of lovers escape from the magical
parent of the girl by throwing behind them a
series of toilet accessories which turn into
physical obstacles to delay pursuit. Nilsson

too sees in the device of Medea to delay her father by cutting up her small brother and throwing the pieces overboard one by one, a rationalized version of *The Magical Flight.* It may be so, but the rationalization has then effected a pretty extensive change. But the alternative form of this story, *The Transformation Flight,* in which the lovers escape pursuit by a series of metamorphoses (Grimm 51, 56) does seem to have left traces in the story of the elopement of Zeus with Aegina. The angry father, Asopus, learned from Sisyphus, who had seen them from his lofty perch at Acro-Corinth, of the flight of the lovers; thereupon Zeus turned Aegina into the island of that name and himself into a stone.

The story of how Daedalus hurled his nephew, who had aroused his professional jealousy by the invention of the saw, from the cliff of the Acropolis, is undoubtedly a variant of one form of a widespread legend of *The Jealous Architect and his Apprentice.*[8] On the other hand the story is one which might well have been invented wherever the peculiarities of the artistic temperament had attracted popular attention.

For identical incidents but in a different setting, there is the ruse by which a hero sets stupid magical persons to fight and destroy each other by throwing a stone into their midst and inducing them to quarrel (Grimm 20). This is how Cadmus dealt with the warriors who sprang from the dragon's teeth, and from the Cadmus story the episode probably passed into the Argonaut saga. But this secondary form seems to go back as early as Eumelus, and was therefore current in Europe before the second half of the eighth century B.C. It has therefore a very respectable European antiquity, if we may regard the incident as distinctive. Rejuvenation by cutting up the old man and boiling the pieces (Medea and Aeson) occurs in a different context in stories of the type of Grimm 81.

The variant forms of the *Aedon* story contain some interesting incidents. The story itself is a " Just-so story " to explain the peculiarities of the swallow, the nightingale, the woodpecker and so on, though I think myself that it has been modelled upon a type of hieratic myth connected with very early and barbaric ritual. You will remember the common tale of how the clever member of a band of brothers or sisters, when sleeping at an ogre's house, changes their nightcaps, night clothes or positions in the bed, with the result that the ogre kills his own children in mistake. In the version of the *Aedon* story which was used by Euripides in his *Ino* the nightclothes, in Pherecydes the caps, and in a variant given by the scholiast the positions of the children were changed.

Again, in Antoninus Liberalis, the wrongs of Chelidonis are made known by her telling them to the water-vessel; compare Grimm, Nos. 89, 91. In the *Tereus* of Sophocles, Philomela published her plight by weaving the story on a cloth. The peculiarity of this method of conveying the news of incarceration or of injury unjustly received is that it is rather characteristically oriental. In Eastern stories it occurs frequently, often to point the moral of the value for everyone to learn a trade, as the Ottoman Sultans, for example, were required by custom to do.

All the correspondences which we have so far noticed, are interesting enough in themselves, but the similarities are hardly sufficiently detailed or elaborate to bear the weight of argument, which is sometimes put upon them. Let me now take an instance of an unquestionable debt. The external soul meets us again in the purple lock of Nisus of Megara and with it is bound up the tale of *The Treacherous Maiden*. A king is being besieged and is invincible so long as his life token is intact. His daughter either for love of the besieging captain or for gold betrays him. The victor spurns her and puts her to death; in some versions she is crushed by the weight of the gold or of the bracelets or shields of the victorious soldiery. I know seven classical heroines of this tale (Scylla, Comaetho, Peisidice, Arne, Demonice, Polycrite, Tarpeia). Gibbon alludes to a version, attached to a Mesopotamian war, in a Byzantine writer, and the *Gesta Romanorum* has taken another from the Lombard histories of Paulus Diaconus. It is current today in the Levant as a frequent though not invariable (e.g., with Leander's tower on the Bosporus, the Turkish name for which is Kiz Kulesi, a variant of the *Maid of the Mill* is associated) explanation of the not uncommon place-name, *The Maiden's Castle*. That these stories and legends are all connected I have the less doubt because I believe that even the classical variants are not genuine folktales in origin, but are derived from literary invention. Though repudiated by native tradition in Megara, the story of

[97]

Scylla's betrayal of her father's purple lock is alluded to by Aeschylus, but there is no hint in his allusion of the love-interest. This, there is reason to think, the story owes to the romantic literary taste of the Hellenistic age, when it first achieved its great popularity and became a model for imitation.

There are, however, some complete series of genuine folktale incidents in classical mythology, which recur in European folktales. *Odysseus and Polyphemus* must have been already current as a folktale when Homer made use of it for the *Odyssey*. Forms of it are widely distributed both in the medieval story books and in modern collections. It has been incorporated in the *Arabian Nights* and is found in modern Persia — a poor version has even reached Korea — but the literary history of the story in the Middle Ages and the character and distribution of the modern variants seem to me to make it quite certain that the tale is of European, not of Indian, origin.

The story of how Zeus sent Death to Sisyphus, but how that cunning ruffian succeeded in tying Death up, thereby bringing the course of nature to a temporary standstill, was known to the author of the *Iliad*. A variant of it forms part of Grimm 82. It too would seem definitely European.

European again I believe to be the story of *Polyidus and the Snakes* (duplicates were told in antiquity of Tylo and of Ptolemy, son of Lagus) which is a variant of part of Grimm 16. Polyidus, it will be remembered, was immured in a tomb with the dead son of Minos. He killed a snake and observed how another snake laid a leaf upon its fellow and restored it to life. By the use of this herb he then resurrected the boy.

The earlier part of Grimm 16 may remind us of a story, which was extremely popular in the medieval books and was eventually to supply material for Voltaire's *Zadig, the Widow of Ephesus*. This first occurs in Petronius, but I am far from confident that it is not of oriental origin, for it appears early in oriental literature and belongs to a rather characteristic oriental group of stories. Further by the time of Petronius oriental stories, though not in their later profusion, were already beginning to filter through to Europe.

That the famous tale of *Cupid and Psyche* in Apuleius, though it has been dressed up by the author, is genuinely a folktale, not a mere allegory, there can be no doubt whatever. It is a variant in fact of Grimm 88. The forms of this story are legion, and between them they cover the whole Indo-European area. I am myself of opinion that the version followed by Apuleius is European in origin.

On the other hand, the story of *The Master Thief and the King's Treasury* is told by Herodotus as an Egyptian story. It was told also in Greece of Trophonius and Agamedes as early as the last of the cyclic poets, Eugammon of Cyrene. In India it occurs early and is popular, and it is one of the stories which passed with Buddhism from India into China.[9] As we shall presently see, I am inclined to suggest that the original home of the story was in Egypt and that it passed thence on the one hand to Greece and on the other to the East. But about this hypothesis we shall have more to say, when we have taken a glance at the problem of the fable.

Fables and drolls still remain to be considered. That drolls were current in antiquity there can be very little doubt, and the Athenians will have enjoyed popular stories at the expense of the Boeotian "pigs," as they called their slower witted neighbours, not unlike those which are told by the modern Greeks about the men of Chios, which is the Gotham of the Asia Minor coast. A series of proverbial sayings about noodles such as Morichus, Praxilla, Meletius, or Margites, who would not touch his wife for fear that she would complain to her mother, shows that stories of the general character of *The Three Sillies* were current in antiquity. The so-called *Sybaritic Tales* probably belonged to the genre of drolls, but unfortunately we know very little about their actual contents.

With regard to fables we are more fortunate. Aesop, the alleged father of the European fable, was reputed to have been a Phrygian slave, who belonged to a Samian master in the sixth century B.C. Whether Aesop was really an historical person or not, is of as little importance for our purpose as the question whether Joe Miller was a real or fictitious character. For once the Aesop tradition was started, all fables were fathered upon him, and, what in reality is a story frame, the *Life of Aesop* prefaced to the fables, began to be built up out of folklore material.

The fables of Aesop became very popular in the fifth century B.C., as is shown by numerous allusions to them in Aristophanes. Socrates in prison contemplated turning Aesop into verse, but the first collection actually published in book form was that of Demetrius of Phalerum at the beginning of the third century B.C. This collection has been lost, and the Aesop, which we know, goes back through a series of medieval collections, which will be found enumerated in Jacobs' edition of Caxton's *Aesop*, to Phaedrus in the first century after Christ and Babrius in the third, a Greek who wrote in Latin and a Latin who wrote in Greek. *The Life of Aesop* in the older editions will be found to be attributed to the fifteenth-century scholar Planudes, but that it was already in the process of formation in the fifth century B.C. is clear from the allusions of Herodotus, and references to incidents from it occur in later classical authors. Probably Planudes' version is substantially a Hellenistic compilation; except, however, for incidents, which can be identified by external evidence, we cannot be sure how old may be the other parts of a popular romance, which has grown by accretion.

Many primitive peoples tell beast stories; in the continent of Africa, whence Uncle Remus'

forbears took them to America, they are especially popular. To look for a single original
inventor or even an original home for the beast
fable would probably be to chase a Will o' the
Wisp. The fable, as the story of Abimelech reminds us, was early known among the He-
brews, and even in Greek literature it occurs
before the supposed date of Aesop. Hesiod
quotes the fable of *The Hawk and the Nightingale* and Archilochus *The Eagle and the Fox*
(Aesop 5), *The Monkey and the Fox* (Aesop
44), and possibly *The Lion's Den*, (Aesop 243),
which was certainly known to Solon. The monkey, of which the passage in Archilochus is the
first mention in European literature, is not native to Greece, and it is reasonable to suppose
that this story reached the Greeks from some
land where apes were indigenous. For though
the practice of telling beast stories may have
developed independently in different parts of
the world, it is difficult to believe that particular fables were invented more than once.

Here lies the great importance of the literary history of Aesop, for there are a number
of correspondences between the fables of Aesop
and Indian beast stories. In the East an important fable literature was early put together,

because the fable was used as a vehicle of Buddhist instruction. The *Jatakas* or *Birth Stories of Buddha* are collections of stories, which purport to be experiences which had happened to the Buddha in the course of his previous animal incarnations and were narrated by him to his disciples to illustrate ethical precepts. It is very unfortunate that the earliest literary source for these *Birth Stories* does not seem to be older than the fifth century after Christ. It is usually supposed, however, that this is an accident of manuscript tradition, that the *Birth Stories* are very ancient and may in substance go back to the teaching of Buddha himself (fifth century B.C.), who adapted a popular form of storytelling for the purposes of his teaching much as Christ made use of the parable. Some support is lent to this view by the fact that certain reliefs upon early Buddhist temples in Ceylon show that at least some of the *Birth Stories* existed in the same form, in which we have them in the written records, at least two centuries earlier. Although, therefore, it is quite true that Pausanias' version of the *Beth Gellert* story is earlier as a literary record than the version in the *Jatakas*, we cannot, if this hypothesis is

correct, draw the conclusion that the Greek is
the older story and that the tale has travelled
from Greece to India.

It seems to me that there is a good deal of
probability in the current view that the *Jatakas*
are by many centuries older in substance than
the oldest literary record of them which we
possess, and that at any rate the safest plan
for the present is to accept their great antiquity as a working hypothesis, remembering, of
course, that it is nothing more.[10]

The problem then arises, what is the relation
between the stories which are common to Aesop
and to Buddhist India? As regards the *Aesop*
of Planudes, it is obvious that there has been
ample opportunity for direct contact between
Europe and the East, which might enable the
stories to be transmitted to and fro. If we then
go back to Babrius and Phaedrus, the far-
Eastern trade under the Roman empire provided a channel by which the exchange of
stories was possible, and earlier still the Alexandria of the Ptolemies was a center where
East and West met and mingled. In point of
fact characteristically oriental incidents can be
traced in Strabo and Aelian, and long ago
Rohde showed that oriental stories of the *Sin-*

bad the Sailor type were known in Alexandria and affected the form of Hellenistic romance. But when we turn back further to the period which preceded the conquests of Alexander, it becomes more difficult to account for a cultural contact which would have enabled Greece and India to interchange stories. Nevertheless it is certain that fables and stories which are common to Greece and India were current in the Greek world before Demetrius published his collection of *Aesop's Fables,* for the fortunate accident of allusions to specific fables in Aristophanes and other Greek writers has provided us with some actual examples.

Such are *Eagle and Fox* (Archilochus, Aristophanes), *Eagle and Dungbeetle* (Aristophanes), *Weasel as Bride* (Strattis), *Dog and Shadow* (Democritus). We may notice also two oriental stories in Herodotus: the story of *Intaphernes' Wife,* ostensibly a Persian story, which Sophocles in the *Antigone* no doubt took over from his friend, and the *Tale of Hippocleides.* The first, the point of which is that a woman is prepared to sacrifice husband and children rather than a brother, because in the course of nature the former can be replaced, but the latter cannot, occurs, clearly from a common source, both in the *Jatakas* and in the epic *Ramayana*. The second has been shown to be a version, and surely a secondary version, of *The Dancing Peacock* in the *Jatakas*.[11]

Clearly these early similarities demand explanation. Direct contact between India and Greece before Alexander there was none; indirect contact can only have been affected through the Middle East. Of a drift in some of our stories from East to West there are certain indications. Even Hesiod's father came from Cyme on the Asiatic coast. Archilochus belonged to the same area, and another lyric poet, Alcaeus, who wrote a poem to his brother who had received a sword of honour from the king of Babylon in recognition of his distinguished services as a mercenary soldier, shows us one channel by which stories might be brought back from Mesopotamia. Aesop is traditionally a native of Asia Minor, and his master was a man of Samos, the home of Pythagoras, which in the sixth century B.C. was the principal commercial state in the Egyptian trade. In Herodotus, *Intaphernes' Wife* is confessedly Persian, and *Rhampsinitus and the Thief* is Egyptian, while the earlier Greek form of the latter story was recorded by Eugammon of Cyrene in Africa. Again the incident of the prophetic " game of King " in Herodotus' narrative of the childhood of Cyrus is rather characteristically oriental and is connected with the *Child Kadi* motif. Cinnamon, in Herodotus, is used by giant carrion birds for building their nests; the natives put out carcasses, which the birds carry off to their nests, thereby breaking them down with the weight and enabling the watchers to pick up the fragments. This seems to me (a view independently confirmed by the opinion of Rohde) to be a perverted version of the well-known motif of the inaccessible gorge full of precious stones and serpents. The jewels are collected by rolling carcasses into the gorge which giant birds carry off. If they can be made to surrender their prey, jewels will be found sticking to the meat. Forms of this story will be familiar from the adventures of *Sinbad the Sailor;* they occur in the big Indian collections, e.g. Somadeva's *Katha Sarit Sagara,* and run through medieval European literature from Epiphanius (fifth century after Christ) onwards.

There seems, therefore, to be some indication of a drift of certain stories from the East into

Greece in the fifth century and earlier. Immediately, they come from Egypt, Mesopotamia, and Persia. Is it not possible that it was from this area of the Middle East that they passed also to India, that is to say that these early correspondences are to be explained not by Indian stories passing into Greece or Greek into India but by stories passing both into Greece and into India from a common center in the Middle East?

At the present state of our knowledge this theory is purely a guess, though we may hope that new discoveries and the publication of the voluminous papyri which are already waiting in museums to be made accessible to learning, will eventually confirm or refute it. The guess, however, is not intrinsically improbable. A common center from which the influences of popular literature may well have radiated both eastward and westward, is provided by the Persian Empire, which, in the middle of the sixth century B.C., fused into a single cultural unit with a common language, Aramaic, the great nations of the Middle East. The boundaries of this empire extended to the vale of Kashmir, while there was commercial contact with the Indian peoples on the north by the caravan routes and on the south by sea through the Persian Gulf.

The difficulty in testing our hypothesis arises from the almost total loss of the secular popular literature of the ancient Middle East. Except for the contents of a few Egyptian papyri and the fragments of secular tradition which have chanced to become incorporated in the canon of the Old Testament, and one other very important exception, we are completely ignorant of its content. This exception is the romance known as *The Words of Ahikar,* of which versions, derived from some common prototype, exist in a large number of languages. Although Clement of Alexandria states that Democritus had translated *Ahikar* into Greek from a Babylonian original, it was the general view until recently that this attribution was fraudulent, and that the work, Greek or Jewish in origin, was a compilation of the Hellenistic age and not much older than the *Book of Tobit* in which allusions to it occur. Now Ahikar contains some property in common with *Aesop's Fables* and *The Life of Aesop.* Upon the old view this was naturally explained as having been taken from the Greek *Aesop* by the compilers of *Ahikar.* But a few years ago a fragmentary and poor version of *Ahikar* was discovered among the Aramaic papyri at Elephantine, showing that the book was actually in popular circulation among the Jewish garrison at that frontier fortress of Egypt as early as the fifth century B.C. The antiquity of the book was thus vindicated, and the best opinion appears to assign a Mesopotamian origin to the prototype of this Aramaic version. It follows that the tradition about Democritus may well be true after all, and that *Aesop* may just as well have borrowed from *Ahikar* as *Ahikar* from *Aesop*.

Following this up, Smend re-examined the fables which are common to the two and showed that in some cases the Aesopic version seemed definitely to be an adaptation or secondary version of the one in *Ahikar*. One of these, Aesop's *The Goat and the Vine,* in which the fable in *Ahikar* has clearly been altered and its point blunted in order to adapt it to a peculiarity of Greek sacrificial ritual, can be dated as early as the beginning of the third century B.C. when Leonidas of Tarentum made a famous epigram out of it. It is therefore reasonable to suppose that it was included in the first collected edition of the *Fables* by Demetrius of Phalerum. I should myself guess that the *Ahikar* version was translated into Greek by Democritus, and that the Aesopic adaptation may have been made by Theophrastus, the master and friend of Demetrius, who wrote an elaborate treatise upon sacrificial rites, and among whose lost papers an " Achikaros " is recorded.[12]

My view about the whole matter is this, though it cannot be stated as more than a probability, because of the defective nature of the evidence. A certain number of folktales, though not a very large number, were certainly current in classical antiquity in much the same form, in which they are today current in Europe.[13] There are further a very large number of general ideas and isolated incidents which are common to classical antiquity and to modern European folktale, but the incidents occur in a different context and the correspondence does not extend over a connected series of episodes. The general practice is to take these, and to suppose the existence of original versions of stories analogous to the modern ones in which they are found, and to explain the difference of context by supposing that the modification necessary to adapt them to the specific purposes

of mythology is the cause of it. I do not myself
believe that, where the evidence is already so
defective and difficult to handle, these adventures into the realms of pure speculation are
very profitable, nor do they make sufficient
allowance for the chances of coincidence and
the hopeless vagueness of generic similarities
of primitive ideas for purposes of identification and classification. Further the very marked
influence of oriental forms of story telling upon
modern European folktales seems to me unde-
niable. There are curious correspondences between classical and Indian stories before Alexander. If the Indian stories are as old as the
orientalists claim, I should suggest that this
may be due to a diffusion of stories eastward
and westward from a common center in the
Persian Empire. After Alexander, Alexandria,
and, later, the Eastern contacts of the Roman
empire provided means of transmission, and I
do not think that it would be difficult to show
that the number of oriental motifs, say in
Aelian, supported this view. But it was in the
Middle Ages that the big Indian collections
were first translated into Persian and Arabic,
and through these media they were transmitted
to Europe. They caught the popular taste and

spread throughout Europe, not merely by oral transmission, but in the more permanent form of literature. Further from the *Dolopathos* or the *Gesta Romanorum* onwards, European literature of one form or another has never ceased to repeat them and keep them alive. It is to this fact that I should attribute their vitality and the predominance, which seems to me unquestionable, of the oriental types over the tales indigenous to Europe.

IV. THE CLASSICAL AND THE
MEDIEVAL TRADITIONS

THE brief outline of the history of classical civilization which was given in our first chapter, will have suggested that the contact of the medieval world was not with ancient Greek culture; with Greek thought, that is to say, at the height of its power and achievement. That did not effectively influence European culture until the re-discovery of Greek letters at the Renaissance. The classical tradition in the West which persisted was the Hellenistic, transmitted through the channels of the later Latin writers. Further, before the collapse of the Western Empire there had been a long and steady decline of rationalism, a slow continuous process which began as early as the influence of Posidonius in the first century B.C., and of which the medieval attitude of mind is the inevitable conclusion. Credulity gradually ousted rationalism. Stoicism, which had disastrously accepted astrology as the necessary consequence of its physical conception of the nature of the universe as a finite organism of which the earth was the center, became increasingly coloured by religious emotion and superstitious belief. Neo-Platonism developed the speculations of Plato's *Timaeus* into a systematic demonology. Intermediate spiritual agents in the new Platonism served to bridge the difficult gulf which the Platonic theory of absolute " ideas " had left between the separated worlds of Appearance and Reality. This doctrine provided the basis for a general belief in the incessant interference of omnipresent supernatural agencies in the ordinary affairs of life. This in turn produced a habit of mind which regarded it as more probable that a given phenomenon should have a spiritual or supernatural than a natural cause.

An age of erudition but of very little creative power professed an increasing respect for antiquity and authority. The growing popularity of allegory, which the Stoics had first brought into general use in order to reconcile their philosophic conception of the nature of God and the universe with the continued practice of pagan religion, assisted in discounting the value of practical experience and common sense. It came to be considered that an obvious

could not be a true meaning, but that behind
the obvious, there must lurk some deep esoteric
significance. Long before the fall of the Western Empire reason, though not reasoning, had
been dethroned. The reasoning indeed remains
subtle, the arguments are often sound, and, at
any rate when we come to the great medieval
masters, there is no lack of mental power. It
is the premises, not the logical methods, that
are at fault in the later classical and medieval
learning, and this in turn is due to uncritical
respect for authority and a taste for the marvellous and the irrational, the spirit of *credo
quia impossibile*, which led indiscriminate erudition to perpetuate and emphasize precisely
what was worthless in the inheritance of learning, and relatively to neglect the submission of
its postulates to the test of practical experi-
ment.

This world of declining rationalism had become Christian, but the intellectual conse-
quences from our point of view were negligible
one way or the other. The early Christians
were men of their time and shared its intellectual weaknesses. The demonology of Christian
Fathers does not differ in essentials from that
of pagan Neo-Platonists; the Christian devils

and angels merely step into the shoes of the good and bad *daemons* of the pagans. Again the Christian use or abuse of allegory is no better nor worse than that of the later Stoics nor are its results less fantastic. To take but one familiar example, you may read in the headings to the chapters in the authorized version of the Bible the explanation of the love song called *The Song of Songs* in terms of an allegory of Christ and his Church.

Although these changes in mental outlook were gradual and continuous, there is normally acceleration upon a downward slope. The gulf between medieval learning and Greek science at its best is wide indeed, and both the lapse of time and the political disintegration of the Roman Empire increasingly distorted the popular idea of the character of ancient civilization. Of its grandeur the ordinary man, say in the XIIth century, had no doubt, but its character he discerned strangely refracted through the medium of certain pre-conceived ideas. The ancients he knew were heathens, not Christians; they had been both idolators and worshippers of devils. Here he but followed the Christian Fathers, who, seizing upon the indiscreet admission of the Platonists that some daemons were evil, had maintained not that the pagan gods were empty fabrications of the fancy, but that they were evil spirits. This view lingered even among the learned into the nineteenth century, for Rawlinson, the great translator of Herodotus, thought that the responses of the oracle at Delphi were uttered by an evil spirit.

The grandeur that was Rome was therefore, plausibly enough, attributed to the magical skill of these mighty men of the past with the assistance of their demons. Apart from political tradition, there were two main witnesses to this mighty past, books and monuments. Some of the great works of the ancient poets, Ovid's *Metamorphoses,* Statius' *Thebaid,* or Virgil's *Aeneid* were still read by men of learning. But their contents had also been made accessible to a wider public in romances, in which the old material had been worked up in a new form consonant with the medieval imagination. This, like that of children, had little sense of historical change and conceived the figures of the ancient world as moving against a background of circumstances like their own. Aeneas becomes a worthy knight and Virgil, a learned clerk; Dido and the romantic love interest take on a new importance.

But apart from this literary witness there was ocular testimony to the greatness of the ancient civilization in the archaeological remains, of which in particular Rome and Constantinople were full. These impressed popular imagination less with their aesthetic or historical interest than with their supposedly magical origin and purpose. For these idols had either been the habitations of the ancient gods or they were instruments of enchantment. That is primarily the view of the antiquities of Rome which the medieval pilgrim found expressed in the curiously mixed and imaginative information which was contained in his guide book to the monuments, the *Mirabilia Urbis Romae*. The same attitude is characteristic of similar Byzantine treatises on the monuments of Constantinople of Codinos and Choniates. There the tradition was simply taken over by the Turks, and we find a similar list of talismans given by the Turkish Evliya Effendi in the XVIIth century. An example of how widely the popular imagination was impressed by these remains is shown for instance by the popular English ballad of *King Arthur and King Cornwall*, which is derived from a *chanson de geste* relating the visit of King Charle-

magne to Constantinople and the wondrous
magical machinery of the emperor's palace
there. The view that antique monuments are
magical is not dead today. To take but one example, there is the Corinthian colonnade at
Salonica to which the resident Spanish Jews
have given the name *Incantadas*, "the en-
chanted figures."

Of course people knew that though some of
these talismans might be prophetic and their
efficacy remained to be tested, there were
others which were no longer active, and they
were conscious too that the remains of antiquity were often mutilated and had certainly
been more numerous than they now were. But
this was accounted for by the belief, which is
expressed for instance in Milton's *Hymn to the
Nativity*, that at the Birth of Christ the pagan
gods and pagan magic fell and ceased to func-
tion, or the corresponding Moslem tradition
that at the birth of the Prophet their virtue left
the ancient idols.[14]

The religion of the heathen was thought of
as idolatrous magic; the most useful part of
magic is the power to foretell the future and
in what may be called practical magic, divination will always be found to be prominent. As

a result ancient religion was thought of as primarily oracular and the oracles as having functioned by means of speaking images, a view which coloured classical scholarship well into the XVIIIth century. The shape of the Pantheon at Rome led to the general belief that the normal form of a classical temple was a round building, surrounded inside by a row of statues. The superstition that every round church is necessarily placed upon the site of a classical temple is still rife among the local antiquaries of Europe.

Both in the East and in the West the names of great men of antiquity survived in the popular memory, but just as the *Aeneid* was transmogrified into a medieval romance, so the character of the great authors was metamorphosed by medieval imagination. These great wise men had been enchanters and a series of legends derived from folklore material collected around them. The most famous of such histories is the medieval life of the enchanter Virgil. The material for what thus became a popular romance was mainly put together by the scholastics, such as Neckham, John of Salisbury, or Gervase of Tilbury who systematized popular legends and recollections of classical learning into a composite whole.

Further, some of these wise men of the past, either because of their greatness and goodness, e.g. Trajan for his justice to the widow, or because of their supposed prophecies about Christianity, e.g. Virgil's *Messianic Eclogue,* or because of a common moral sentiment, which as early as the end of the second century had led Tertullian to speak of "our Seneca" and by the fourth century had given rise to the forged *Correspondence of Seneca and St. Paul,* were popularly supposed either to have been partially Christians, where an acquaintance with chronology necessitated bringing in the doctrine of progressive revelation, or else to have become wholly Christians by conversion. Hence the Christian Sibyl, who adds her witness to that of David, the Christian Augustus, or that sweet Christian poet Statius.

The same sort of thing happened also in the Moslem world, which retained similarly distorted memories of the Greek men of learning. The enchanter Iflatoun (Plato) is still locally held to have been responsible for draining the plain of Konia. Among Evliya's magicians we meet with Apollonius of Tyana, Galen, Hippocrates, Aristotle, and Pythagoras, and it is notorious that the Alexander of Hellenistic romance fired the imagination of the East more permanently even than it did that of the West. We may notice too that Evliya speaks of Fisaghorat (Pythagoras) as "the Unitarian," i.e. he anticipated the Moslem doctrine of the Unity of God and was partially a Mohammedan before Mohammed, just as Virgil was partially a Christian before Christ.

Although the belief in talismanic statues was thus fostered by the medieval view of archaeology, it had been a growing force in the declining classical world. Already in the first century B.C. Sulla, that strange compound of scepticism and superstition, went nowhere without a little image of Apollo. In the second, third, and fourth centuries after Christ, as magic became more and more the vogue, it became also more and more elaborate. Inevitably an increasing importance attached to magical paraphernalia, as any reader of the magical papyri will recognize. Conjuring apparatus became more and more cunningly devised by the impostors who everywhere flourish in a society with magical leanings, and the account of fraudulent apparatus which is preserved in the polemic of Hippolytus does not differ in character from the description by Reginald Scot in *The Discoverie of Witchcraft* of that which was employed in his day to couzen the simple.

This increased vogue of formal magic and the apotheosis of its apparatus prepared the way for the medieval interpretation of archaeology which we have noticed, and for the great popularity of the talisman both in the East and in the West. The word talisman itself is probably not derived, as is generally supposed, from the Arabic *tilsam*, Turkish *tilisim*. Both the Arabic and the European forms are almost certainly independent and parallel derivatives from the common source in the past participle passive of the Greek τελῶ , " to do " or " perform," in the specialized sense of " to perform magical rites," a usage with which we may compare the threat of the witch in *Macbeth*, " I'll do, and I'll do, and I'll do."

Medieval talismans were mainly of five kinds. Either they concealed or contained or in some way guarded the luck of the city or the empire. Constantine, for instance, was known to have placed both the Palladium of old Rome and also a mixed assortment of Christian relics beneath the column in his new city. Relics were increasing in popularity in the later paganism, and here Christianity took over much of pagan custom and beliefs. As an example, we might compare the pagan tombs in Asia Minor, which have a tomb beneath and a shrine above, with the Christian counterpart of a tomb below and a reliquary above, like that described by Gregory of Nazianzus in an epigram: " One structure this, but tomb beneath and shrine above; tomb for its builders, shrine for the martyrs."

Other antique statues were supposed to have been erected on the principle of "like cures like " (we might compare the Brazen Serpent erected by Moses in the wilderness), a bronze gnat to keep gnats away, a scorpion to prevent a plague of scorpions, or a stork to get rid of storks.

Others again served to imprison bad luck or diseases, which were held fast in captivity so long as the monument remained undisturbed. In modern Athens there is a square, which is never known by its official name but always as *Colonaki,* because beneath the column in it a number of diseases have thus been securely imprisoned.

Others again guarded secret treasures, like

that in the well-known story which is told, amongst others, of Gervase and of Virgil, of the subterranean treasury lighted by a carbuncle at which the statue of an archer is aiming his arrow. The folly of the intruders allows the statue to discharge its arrow, the vault is plunged in darkness, and the adventurers escape with difficulty ere worse befalls.

Others served as ordeals, like the *Bocca della Verità* at Rome, which was really a slab carved like a mouth, which had formed the covering for an ancient drain. If a person with his hand within its jaws committed perjury, the hand was bitten off. With this type of talisman is associated the story of the clever ruse by which a lady who has been guilty of infidelity, when forced to face the ordeal, escapes by framing an ambiguous oath.

An interesting piece of literary evidence for the growing taste for talismans may perhaps be noticed. In the XIIth century the Byzantine Eumathius or Eustathius wrote a feeble copy of the novel of Achilles Tatius. Now in Achilles there is a virginity test, in which a magical spring rises and covers the forsworn. In the insipid Byzantine imitation the spring has been improved by the addition of a magical statue

of Artemis, which bends its bow, if the girl has
been guilty.

The better I become acquainted with the literature of the late classical period, the more I
am struck with the continuity of the literary
tradition which ultimately did so much to
mould the popular religious and superstitious
legends of Europe. How 'medieval' is the romance of Philostratus *In Honour of Apollonius
of Tyana!* The genre, to begin with, is that of
the *aretalogy*, that is to say a collection of wonderful stories to the credit of an exorcist and
prophet, which will serve both to confirm the
faith of believers and to provide them simultaneously with entertainment. The Christian
counterpart to this pagan type of literature is
provided by the *Apocryphal Acts of the Apos-
tles* and the *Lives of the Saints,* literary works,
it may be mentioned, which exercised a far
greater influence upon popular belief and
legend than is often recognized. The court at
Babylon, which Apollonius visits, is distinguished by magical images of wrynecks which
sing, just like the mechanical wonders for
which Constantinople was famous in the *chanson de geste.* Again the king of the Indians has
magical automata, which on the one hand go

[128]

back to the living images of the legendary
Daedalus and also to the satires of Attic com-
edy upon the comforts of "The Golden Age,"
and upon the other hand remind us of the automata of Simon Magus in the *Clementine Rec-
ognitions* or the animated statuary which was
later attributed to medieval masters of the
magical art. At Gades Apollonius saw a talisman, a speaking statue of Themistocles. His
exorcism of the evil spirit, which then over-
turned an adjacent statue as a sign of its exit,
can be exactly paralleled in the *Apocryphal
Acts*.

If we turn to the natural sciences we find a
similar continuity. Pliny's *Natural History*, an
amazingly industrious and uncritical collection
of information which has been assembled into a
miscellaneous compendium of knowledge, is at
once the model and the source of most of the
medieval works upon natural science. The type
and much of the specific information is repeated in such analogous compendia as those
of Isidore of Seville or Hildegarde of Bingen.
Similarly in Aelian we may notice the begin-
nings of the interpretation of the habits of animals in terms of moral qualities, a distortion of
natural history more silly than but not different

in kind from Plutarch's view of history as a gallery of moral examples of vice and virtue, which leads through the *Physiologus* to the allegorical nonsense of the medieval *Bestiaries*. In the same way the medieval *Lapidaria*, or treatises on the occult virtues of precious stones, go back through Epiphanius' treatise *On the Gems in the Breastplate of the High Priest* to the Elder Pliny and his congeners.

"Some of Galen's works," says Dr. Singer, "are mere drug lists, little superior to those of Dioscorides; with the depression of the intelligence that corresponded with the break up of the Roman Empire, it was these that were chiefly seized on and distributed in the West. Attractive, too, to the debased intellect of the late Roman world were certain spurious, superstitious, and astrological works that circulated in the name of Galen and Hippocrates."[15] Thanks to the prevailing interest in the marvellous, the increasing belief in the greater probability of magical than of natural causation, and the complete confusion of moral and religious with scientific issues in the interpretation of nature, this perpetuation of the mistakes rather than the triumphs of the learning of the past was unfortunately the rule. Thus Aristotle's work as a naturalist was discarded; his biological method and some of his individual discoveries have been rediscovered only in recent times. Aristotle's mistaken notions of physics and physiology, which were themselves due to a neglect of the methods of direct personal observation, which made him so great a naturalist, were perpetuated as axioms. In Persia, diseases are still classified by their humours, are divided into hot and cold and damp and dry, and are treated accordingly.

Certain magical remedies persisted right through the Middle Ages, and, as my colleague, Dr. Dilling, informs me, many ingredients in the ordinary prescriptions of our pharmacopoeia today are quite worthless if harmless relics of classical antiquity. The supposed efficacy of such remedies is often based upon the magical principle that "like cures like." Thus, ever since Andromachus, the physician of Nero, the recipe for theriac, a specific against snake-bite and poison, has had for its chief constituent the flesh of vipers. Another antidote, the earth of Lemnos, the famous *terra sigillata* of medicine, was sold in sealed packets in the time of Pliny. Its use has a rather curious history.[16] Between

the late classical period and the XVIth century
there is no evidence that the doctors of the West
had any first-hand acquaintance with Lemnos
and the genuine earth. But *Terra Lemnia* continued to be prescribed, and so dear was the
alleged article of commerce that Maimonides in
the XIIth century could propose powdered
emeralds as a substitute! In the XVIth century,
when the Spanish Jews settled in Turkey, there
was a great revival. The earth was annually ex-
cavated with a solemn religious ceremony and
was exported by the Turks. It was still, of
course, a monopoly and consequently dear, and
it is interesting to find that one of the attrac-
tions set forth in Heriot's *Report of Virginia*
(1558), is the prospect of finding equally effec-
tive substitutes for the genuine earth of Lemnos, in the New World.

Where modern peasant folklore agrees with
ancient medicine it is not always easy to know
whether the recipe has filtered down from the
tradition of the learned or has a local and independent origin. Thus Pliny records two
kinds of magical snake-stone. One, the adders'
egg, is made by a congress of snakes at Mid-
summer, who collect and blow the stone from
their spume; the other is a bezoar obtained

from the head of serpents or dragons. The first
Pliny had from the Druids, the second from
Eastern sources. Both persist in the medieval
tradition. The adders' egg exactly corresponds
to the Cornish *milpreve* or the Welsh *maen
magl* (spotted stone) of modern superstition.
Since Pliny heard of it from the Druids, it may
may well be Celtic in origin. Nevertheless it is
possible that learned tradition may have something to do with its perpetuation even in Wales,
if *magl*, as I am informed, is a rare loan word
from the Latin *macula*.

Chester in *Love's Martyr* says of the swallow:

> *His yong ones being hurt within the eies,*
> *He helps them with the herb calcedonies.*

The idea that if young swallows or serpents
were blinded, their eyes grew again, is as old as
Aristotle. Pliny tells us that the herb celandine
is used by the parent birds for the purpose.
Was Chester's information of erudite or of
popular origin? Similarly the plant *dracun-
culus* is recommended by Pliny as a cure for
snake-bite; *dragontia* or snakeweed is one of
the regular remedies of medieval learning; in

modern Leicestershire *viper's bugloss* is a popular specific. Is this folk recipe due to learned tradition or is it merely the product of the independent application of the "like cures like" principle, which has led the peasants of Leicestershire also to use a plant which resembles a snake for snake-bite?

Of witches and the practices of Black Magic we have said something in the second chapter. When Piso was accused of murdering Germanicus, Tacitus tells us that "there were found hidden in the floor and in the walls of his room disinterred remains of human bodies, incantations, and spells, and the name of Germanicus inscribed on leaden tablets, half burnt cinders smeared with blood and other horrors by which in popular belief souls are devoted to the gods below." The leaden tablets are those which are technically known as *defixionum tabellae*. A spell against a person was inscribed upon a small sheet of lead, which was then placed in a grave or nailed to the wall of a tomb. The practice possibly came from the East; it took firm root in Attica in the fourth century B.C.; thence it spread later throughout the Roman empire. Hundreds of such spells have been found in various provinces; in

Africa, the land of superstition, they are exceptionally frequent. This precise method is not, I think, characteristic of European witchcraft.

But in general magical methods everywhere much resemble each other, and the magical papyri of the fourth century after Christ present a good many analogies to medieval magic. Characteristic of them are words of power, which are sometimes Semitic names of God or titles of Egyptian divinities; often they consist of an arrangement of letters of the alphabet, and combinations of the seven vowels, which were supposed to have an affinity with the seven planets, were especially popular. Sometimes they are just gibberish, and sometimes sonorous nonsense words with terminations in *beth* or *oth* to give them the appearance of Egyptian or Oriental words. With these we may perhaps compare an English charm against thieves as quoted by Reginald Scot. *Drochs myroch esenaroth betu baroch ass maaroth.* The gibberish form of charm is at least as old in Latin as the elder Cato, who recommended for a dislocation the use of *huat haut haut istasis tarsis ardannabou dannaustra.* A Roman charm for curing a flux was the following; if

[135]

written out and tied round the middle, the flow of blood will decrease as the word gets shorter:

s i c u c u m a
i c u c u m a
c u c u m a
u c u m a
c u m a
u m a
m a
a

The famous Abracadabra could be somewhat similarly used as a diminishing charm. In the Middle Ages it was inevitable that Latin, the language at once of learning and of religion, should be the most efficient vehicle for charms. *Hocus pocus* is, of course, a corruption of the words of the Mass, *Hoc est corpus meum,* "this is My body." The following, which is recommended by Aubrey in his *Miscellanies* to cure a bite of a mad dog, consists of nonsense words which are intended to sound like Latin. "*Rebus Rubus Epitepscum,* and give it to the Party, or Beast bit, to eat in Bread, or etc. A Gentleman of good Quality, and a sober grave Person, did affirm, that this Receipt never fails."

The witchcraft persecution flourished in Europe mainly between the XIIIth century, when the state employed it as a political weapon against individuals and the Church against heretical sects, and the XVIIth century, when in England the protests of brave men like Reginald Scot mark the beginning of a reaction against an epidemic of hysterical cruelty. But the basis of the proceedings against witches was really laid by the creation of a systematic demonology for the Latin-speaking public of Europe by the scholastics. For it is on the foundation of a pretty rigid and generally accepted theory of witchcraft, that the inquisitors' handbooks, like Sprenger's *Malleus Maleficarum,* are based. Certain classical elements entered into this medieval system of demonology. In particular we may notice the adaptation of Diana-Hecate to be the leader of the witches' revels. The history of this identification must be as follows. Artemis in Greek mythology was the huntress-goddess of the wilds, who was accompanied by a band of attendant nymphs. Already in Greece she had been identified with Hecate, a goddess of magic and the underworld, who might be seen at night at the cross-roads with spectral hounds about her and the company of the dead. Artemis and Hecate were also identified with the Moon. As Diana this composite figure passed into the Roman pantheon, and in later classical antiquity her lunar and ghostly characteristics became more and more emphasized. As a pagan goddess she was for medieval Christians a devil, she was the special patroness of magic and her nocturnal rout exactly fitted the requirements of the witches' sabbath.

Meantime I have omitted to mention the debt of European folklore and superstition to the pseudo-science of the later classical epoch. The printed dream-books which servant girls in most European countries still consult, have been handed down on the same principles as medieval science. For through such medieval dream-books as those of Germanos, Nicephoros, Pseudo-Daniel, and Achmet, they go back in the main to the *Oneirocriticon* of Artemidorus. How far the similar Indian books have been influenced by Artemidorus, I have not sufficient knowledge to judge.[17] The problem is complicated by the fact that Artemidorus himself has included some oriental material in his work and by the consideration that the principles of association and contradiction, upon which, in the long run, all dream interpretation is based, may well have led to the independent invention of similar details in different places. But that Artemidorus' work has dominated the subsequent dream-books of Europe I have little doubt.

What Artemidorus did, was to collect and systematize popular interpretations of dreams. These usually proceed by association (e.g. the loss of a tooth means the death of a close friend or climbing upwards indicates success), or else by contradiction (e.g. to dream of a wedding means a funeral). But in the systematic dream-book, apart from the collection and interpretation of authentic extraordinary dreams, like the long story about playing draughts with Charon which concluded with grass sprouting on the dreamer's thigh, the whole business is elaborated by taking into consideration all the attendant circumstances of the dream. Its meaning will be affected by the sex, status, and profession of the dreamer, the time, day of the week, and season of the year at which the dream occurred, and so on. These complications in fact produce a very intricate if nonsensical system.

Another work of similar character, which

was produced in the late classical period, has had a similar effect upon the folklore of Europe. This is the treatise upon the significance of involuntary motions of the body which, following the habit of the ascription of magical treatises to apocryphal names which is common to the late classical and medieval periods, was said to be the work of the legendary Greek seer Melampus. This Pseudo-Melampus did for the involuntary motions of the body (e.g. tingling of the ear means that someone is speaking of you, or an itching of the palm means that you will receive money) what Artemidorus did for dreams, by prescribing the variations of interpretation which the attendant circumstances in each case necessitate. Diels has collected a number of modern books of a similar character and again I should be inclined to think that much that is in them comes ultimately from Pseudo-Melampus.[18]

The influence of astrology upon science and superstition, until the discoveries of Copernicus and Galileo deprived it of its scientific justification by showing that the universe did not in fact have the earth for its fixed center, is too well known to need elaboration. It may be mentioned in passing that a Greek, Aristarchus of

Samos, actually anticipated their discovery, that the universe was not geo-centric but that the earth diurnally rotated and annually revolved round the sun. Unfortunately his speculations fell flat, mainly because of the quasi-theological hostility of the Stoics, whose whole system rested upon the theory of a geo-centric universe.

The influence of Neo-Platonism, from which the Greek Fathers mainly drew their metaphysics, upon Christian mysticism in all periods would take us rather beyond the scope of our subject, though it would necessarily touch folklore at points. So would the consideration of the great influence which was exercised by Neo-Platonism on the Moslem world. Even a second-hand acquaintance with the Persian poets or with such mystical works as the *Mesnevi* of Jellaludin Rumi, the virtual founder of the sect of Bektashi dervishes at Konia, is sufficient to make it clear that a very large element in Sufism and Moslem mysticism has been derived directly from Platonism.

Leaving these great topics, which indeed I am not qualified to handle with authority, I will give one last illustration of the continuity of tradition from early classical folklore through the modifications of the Hellenistic and late classical periods to the medieval and modern world. We all know the description of the Seven Ages of Man which the melancholy Jacques introduces with the image of " All the world's a stage," itself a commonplace of the moralist, the literary ancestry of which can be traced in the diatribes or popular sermons of the Cynics. The number seven had early an importance in Greek folklore, perhaps through the divisions into which the lunar month naturally falls. In the VIth century B.C. a poem of the Athenian statesman Solon divided the life of man upon a septennial system. At seven years the teeth change; at fourteen comes puberty; at twenty-one the beard is grown; twenty-eight is the age of maximum physical strength; thirty-five is the age for marriage and begetting children; at forty-two the character is completely formed; from forty-nine (7 × 7, which therefore became the well-known " climacterical year ") to fifty-six the intellectual faculties are at their best; fifty-six to sixty-three marks a decline; seventy is the natural term of life. In the Hippocratic writings we next find a modification, which divides life into seven periods. First come the stages of infant, boy, youth, and young man,

which end at seven, fourteen, twenty-one, and
twenty-eight respectively; then from twenty-
eight until forty-nine, a period of 3×7 years,
is the adult stage; from forty-nine to fifty-six
we have the senior ($\pi\rho\epsilon\sigma\beta\upsilon\tau\eta\varsigma$; and finally the
seventh stage of old age ($\gamma\epsilon\rho\omega\nu$) from fifty-six
to death. In Hellenistic times the seven ages of
man inevitably became involved with the seven
planets. It was further an essential feature of
Stoic astrology that man was a microcosm, i.e.
a miniature reproduction or model of the universe, a dogma which the Middle Ages took over
from classical antiquity. Now it also came to be
generally believed in the later classical period
that the soul at birth descended to the body
through the planetary spheres, through which it
also reascended after the dissolution of the
body. In its descent it progressively accumulated impurities, which it progressively shed
during its return. The impurities so acquired
were then defined as vices peculiar to each of
the successive planets which it passed, the specific vice of each planet being determined by the
associations of its name. Thus Servius tells us
what Horace knew, that from Saturn the soul
acquires *sloth,* from Mars *anger,* from Venus
lust, from Mercury *avarice,* from Jupiter *ambi-*

tion, from the sun *gluttony,* and from the moon *envy.* We have thus found in classical tradition not only the source of the belief in the climacterical year and the seven ages of man but also the origin of *The Seven Deadly Sins.*[19]

NOTES AND BIBLIOGRAPHY

NOTES

1. The contrary view to mine is developed by J. C. Lawson, *Modern Greek Folklore and Ancient Greek Religion*, Cambridge, England, 1910, pp. 360 foll. and *Classical Review*, XL. 52–58, 116–121 (1926).

2. See W. Schultz, "Das Glück des Lebens in alter Spruchdichtung," in *Laographia*, VII. 100–114 (1923).

3. For the distribution of this proverb see O. Weinreich, *Seneca's Apocolocyntosis*, Berlin, 1923, p. 74; Bolte and Polívka, *Anmerkungen zu den Kinder- und Hausmärchen der Brüder Grimm*, II, p. 372; the classical references are collected in W. Headlam and A. D. Knox, *Herodas, the Mimes and Fragments*, Cambridge, England, 1922, p. 153.

4. The chief protagonist of the extreme oriental theory, in the generation which succeeded Benfey, was the late Emmanuel Cosquin. The notes in his *Contes populaires de Lorraine*, 2 vols., Paris, 1886, are invaluable. Two posthumous volumes, *Les contes Indiens et l'Occident*, Paris, 1922, and *Études Folkloriques*, Paris, 1922, contain not only his latest views but many of his more important contributions to the periodical literature of the subject. English readers will get a useful idea of the indebtedness of Europe to oriental stories from the books of W. A. Clouston, which have further the advantage of being written in an agreeable and interesting style: *The Book of Noodles*, London, 1888; *Eastern Romances and Stories from the Persian, Tamil, Urdu*, Glasgow, 1889; *Popular Tales and Fictions: their Migrations and Transformations*, 2 vols., Edinburgh, 1887.

5. For *exempla* consult T. F. Crane, *The Exempla of Jacques de Vitry*, London, 1890, reprinted 1924; Johannes Pauli, *Schimpf und Ernst*, edited by J. Bolte, Berlin, 1924;

H. Oesterley's is still the best edition of the *Gesta Romanorum*, Berlin, 1871; the last edition of the English translation of Charles Swan, which is known to me, was published in London, 1906 (Editor, W. Hooper). Cf., also, the same in "The Broadway Translations," London and New York. Moses Gaster, *The Exempla of the Rabbis*, London and Leipzig, 1924, contains some useful comparative material. For *fabliaux* see F. H. von der Hagen, *Gesammtabenteuer*, 3 vols., Stuttgart, 1850, which has useful notes and J. Bédier, *Les fabliaux*, Paris, 1895. For folktales in the xviii century see Andrew Lang's introduction to *Perrault's Popular Tales*.

6. For this story see P. Kretschmer, "Das Schwankmärchen von dem Kraut das doppelsichtig macht," in *Laographia*, VII. 18–24 (1923).

7. I have published a more elaborate note upon Perseus and the magical articles in *Journal of the Gypsy Lore Society, Third Series*, III. 151–8 (1924).

8. For the *Architect and Prentice* story see W. Crooke in *Folk-Lore*, XXIX. 219 foll. (1918), and F. W. Hasluck in *Folk-Lore*, XXX. 134–5 (1919).

9. For the distribution of this story see Bolte and Polívka, *op. cit.*, III. pp. 395 foll.

10. For the view that the fable is of oriental origin see Theodor Benfey, *Pantschatantra*, Leipzig, 1859, the introduction to which remains a classic. For an uncompromising defence of Greek priority see Hausrath in Pauly-Wissowa, VI, ii, pp. 1704–1736, s.v. *Fabel*, a good and important article with useful bibliography. Joseph Jacobs' introduction to his edition of *Caxton's Aesop's Fables*, 2 vols., contains a great deal of information but it is mixed with wild speculation.

11. For *Intaphernes' Wife* see R. Pischel, "Zu Sophokles Antigone 909–912," in *Hermes*, XXVIII. 465–8 (1893). For Hippocleides see S. J. Warren, "Herodot vi. 126," in *Hermes*, XXIX. 476–8 (1894), and R. W. Macan, *Herodotus IV–VI*, vol. II, pp. 304–311, London, 1895.

12. For Ahikar see F. C. Conybeare, J. Rendel Harris and Agnes Smith Lewis, *The Story of Ahikar*,[2] Cambridge,

1913, A. E. Cowley, *Aramaic papyri of the Fifth Century B.C.*, translation, etc., Oxford, 1923. For Ahikar and Aesop, R. Smend, " Alter und Herkunft des Achikar Romans und sein Verhältnis zu Aesop," in *Beiheft zur Zeitschrift für die alt-testamentliche Wissenschaft*, XIII, Giessen, 1908. For the fable of *The Goat and the Vine*, W. R. Halliday, in *Annals of Archaeology and Anthropology*, XI. 95–102 (1924).

13. Some examples I have given. The reader may expect, but I am unwilling at the present stage of my investigations to give him a definitive list of such stories. For, to be of practical use, such a catalogue ought to be exhaustive and should also indicate the literary history of each combination of incidents together with some consideration of the setting in which they are found. For example, the Polyidus story is a sufficiently elaborate chain of incidents to be called a story, but its setting in Greek mythology and in Grimm 16 is different. An analysis upon these lines of the common property of classical and Indo-European folktale I have long had in mind and hope, if other occupations allow me the necessary leisure, some day to complete it. I do not know that anyone else has done it; but though it is a longer and more laborious task than perhaps the uninitiated would guess, it is the indispensable prelude to any sound advance in respect of these particular problems.

14. The best idea of how classical antiquity appeared to the medieval mind is most pleasantly acquired by reading Dante. Upon the whole subject of talismans and medieval archaeology see R. M. Dawkins, " Ancient Statues in Medieval Constantinople," in *Folk-Lore*, XXXV. 209–248 (1924). For King Arthur and King Cornwall see F. J. Child, *The English and Scottish Popular Ballads*, No. 30, Vol. I, pp. 274–288.

15. Charles Singer, *Greek Biology and Greek Medicine*, Oxford, 1922, a very good and interesting little book.

16. See F. W. Hasluck, " Terra Lemnia," in *Annual of the British School at Athens*, XVI. 221 foll. (1910).

17. For the oriental dream-book tradition see Julius

von Negelein, *Der Traumschlüssel des Jagaddeva,* Giessen, 1912.

18. H. Diels, " Beiträge zur Zuckungsliteratur des Okzidents und Orients," in *Abhandlungen der königlichen Akademie der Wissenschaften,* 2 vols., Berlin, 1908, 1909.

19. The history of the idea of *The Seven Ages of Man* is treated in detail by Franz Boll, *Die Lebensalter,* Leipzig and Berlin, 1913.

SELECT BIBLIOGRAPHY

I. ENCYCLOPEDIAS, ETC.

DAREMBERG, C., and SAGLIO, E., *Dictionnaire des Antiquités Grecques et Romaines.* 5 vols. Paris, 1877–1919.

HASTINGS, JAS., *Encyclopaedia of Religion and Ethics.* 12 vols. Edinburgh, 1908–1921.

PAULY, A. F. von, WISSOWA, G., KROLL, W., *Real-Encyclopädie der klassischen Altertumswissenschaft.* 13 vols. (incomplete). Stuttgart, 1894–1922.

ROSCHER, W. H., *Ausführliches Lexikon der Griechischen und Römischen Mythologie.* Leipzig, 1885 ff.

Valuable material will be found not only in the journal *Folk-Lore* but also in the volumes of *County Folk-Lore,* which the Folk-Lore Society has issued from time to time.

II. OTHER WORKS

ABT, A., *Die Apologie des Apuleius von Madaura und die antike Zauberei.* Giessen, 1908.

AUBREY, JOHN, *Miscellanies.* London, 1784. *Remaines of Gentilisme and Judaisme,* 1686–7, annotated by J. Britten. Folk-Lore Society, London, 1881.

BAILEY, CYRIL, *Ovid, Fasti, Book III.* Oxford, 1921. *The Religion of Ancient Rome.* London and Chicago, 1907.

BOLTE, J., and POLÍVKA, G., *Anmerkungen zu den Kinder- und Hausmärchen der Brüder Grimm.* Leipzig, 1913–18. Three volumes have appeared; the fourth, which will contain the index, is still awaited.

BRAND, JOHN, *Observations on Popular Antiquities* (edited by Sir H. Ellis). 2 vols. London, 1813. An elaborate new edition of this work is in preparation by the Folk-Lore Society.

[151]

SELECT BIBLIOGRAPHY

BROWNE, SIR THOMAS, *Pseudodoxia epidemica*. A convenient edition is the three-volume edition of the *Works* by C. Sayle. London, 1904–7.

CHILD, FRANCIS JAMES, *The English and Scottish Popular Ballads*. 5 vols. Boston, n.d.

COLLISON-MORLEY, L., *Greek and Roman Ghost Stories*. Oxford, 1912.

COMPARETTI, DOMENICO, *Researches respecting the Book of Sindibad*. Folk-Lore Society, 1882. *Vergil in the Middle Ages*, translated E. F. M. Benecke. London, 1895.

DIETERICH, ALBRECHT, *Kleine Schriften*. Leipzig and Berlin, 1911.

ELWORTHY, FREDERICK THOMAS, *The Evil Eye*. London, 1895.

FAHZ, LUDWIG, *De poetarum Romanorum doctrina magica quaestiones*. Giessen, 1904.

FOWLER, W. WARDE, *The Religious Experience of the Roman People*. London and New York, 1911. *Roman Essays and Interpretations*. Oxford, 1920.

FRAZER, SIR J. G., *Apollodorus: The Library*, with an English translation and commentary, in the *Loeb Classical Library*. 2 vols. London and New York, 1921. *The Golden Bough*, 11 vols. and index. London, 1913–22. *Pausanias's Description of Greece*, translated with commentary. 6 vols. London, 1898.

GOMME, ALICE BERTHA, *Traditional Games of England, Scotland and Ireland*. 2 vols. London, 1894–8.

HALLIDAY, W. R., *Folklore Studies Ancient and Modern*. London, 1924. *Greek Divination*. London, 1913. *Lectures on the History of Roman Religion from Numa to Augustus*. Liverpool, 1921. "Notes upon Indo-European folk-tales and the problem of their diffusion," in *Folk-Lore*, XXXIV. 117–140 (1923). *The Pagan Background of early Christianity*. Liverpool, 1925. Foreword to volume viii of N. M. Penzer, *The Ocean of Story*. London, 1927.

HALLIWELL-PHILIPS, JAMES ORCHARD, (Editor), *Nursery Rhymes of England*.[3] London, 1844. *Popular Rhymes and Nursery Tales*. London, 1841.

SELECT BIBLIOGRAPHY

HARTLAND, EDWIN SIDNEY, *The Legend of Perseus; a study of tradition in story, custom and belief.* 3 vols. London, 1894–6. *The Science of Fairy Tales.* London and New York, 1891.

KÖHLER, REINHOLD, *Kleinere Schriften.* 3 vols. Weimar, 1898–1900.

KUTSCH, F., *Attische Heilgötter und Heilheroen.* Giessen, 1913.

LANG, ANDREW, *Custom and Myth.* New York, 1885. *Myth, Ritual and Religion.*[2] 2 vols. London, 1899. *Perrault's Popular Tales,* edited with introduction and notes. Oxford, 1888.

MARETT, R. R., (Editor), *Anthropology and the Classics.* Oxford, 1908.

MOONEY, JOSEPH J., *Hosidius Geta's tragedy " Medea."* A *Vergilian cento. Latin text and metrical translation. Appended outline of ancient Roman magic.* Birmingham, 1919.

NILSSON, M. P., *A History of Greek Religion.* Oxford, 1925.

PRELLER, L., *Griechische Mythologie,*[4] edited by Karl Robert. Berlin, 1894–1926.

ROHDE, ERWIN, *Der griechische Roman und seine Vorläufer.*[3] Leipzig. 1914. *Psyche; Seelencult u. Unsterblichkeitsglaube der Griechen.*[4] (cf. English translation, in *The International Library of psychology, philosophy and scientific method.* London, 1925.)

ROSE, H. J., *The Roman Questions of Plutarch.* Oxford, 1924. *Primitive Culture in Greece.* London and New York, 1925. *Primitive Culture in Italy.* 1926.

SAMTER, E., *Familienfeste der Griechen und Römer.* Berlin, 1901. *Geburt, Hochzeit und Tod.* Leipzig and Berlin, 1911. *Die Religion der Griechen.* Leipzig, 1914. *Volkskunde im altsprachlichen Unterricht, Teil I, Homer.* Berlin, 1923.

SCOT, REGINALD, *Discoverie of Witchcraft . . .* a reprint of the first edition (1584), edited with notes etc., by B. Nicholson. London, 1886.

[153]

SELECT BIBLIOGRAPHY

SWAINSON, CHARLES, *Provincial names and folklore of British birds*. London, 1885.

TAVENNER, E., *Studies in Magic from Latin Literature*. New York, 1916.

THORNDIKE, LYNN, *A History of Magic and experimental Science during the first Thirteen Centuries of our Era*. 2 vols. New York, 1923.

TYLOR, SIR EDWARD BURNETT, *Primitive Culture*.[4] 2 vols. London, 1903.

WÄCHTER, TH., *Reinheitsvorschriften im griechischen Kult*. Giessen, 1910.

Our Debt to Greece and Rome

AUTHORS AND TITLES

HOMER. *John A. Scott.*

SAPPHO. *David M. Robinson.*

EURIPIDES. *F. L. Lucas.*

ARISTOPHANES. *Louis E. Lord.*

DEMOSTHENES. *Charles D. Adams.*

THE POETICS OF ARISTOTLE. *Lane Cooper.*

GREEK RHETORIC AND LITERARY CRITICISM. *W. Rhys Roberts.*

LUCIAN. *Francis G. Allinson.*

CICERO AND HIS INFLUENCE. *John C. Rolfe.*

CATULLUS. *Karl P. Harrington.*

LUCRETIUS AND HIS INFLUENCE. *George Depue Hadzsits.*

OVID. *Edward Kennard Rand.*

HORACE. *Grant Showerman.*

VIRGIL. *John William Mackail.*

SENECA THE PHILOSOPHER. *Richard Mott Gummere.*

APULEIUS. *Elizabeth Hazelton Haight.*

MARTIAL. *Paul Nixon.*

PLATONISM. *Alfred Edward Taylor.*

ARISTOTELIANISM. *John L. Stocks.*

STOICISM. *Robert Mark Wenley.*

LANGUAGE AND PHILOLOGY. *Roland G. Kent.*

AUTHORS AND TITLES

AESCHYLUS AND SOPHOCLES. *J. T. Sheppard.*

GREEK RELIGION. *Walter Woodburn Hyde.*

SURVIVALS OF ROMAN RELIGION. *Gordon J. Laing.*

MYTHOLOGY. *Jane Ellen Harrison.*

ANCIENT BELIEFS IN THE IMMORTALITY OF THE SOUL. *Clifford H. Moore.*

STAGE ANTIQUITIES. *James Turney Allen.*

PLAUTUS AND TERENCE. *Gilbert Norwood.*

ROMAN POLITICS. *Frank Frost Abbott.*

PSYCHOLOGY, ANCIENT AND MODERN. *G. S. Brett.*

ANCIENT AND MODERN ROME. *Rodolfo Lanciani.*

WARFARE BY LAND AND SEA. *Eugene S. McCartney.*

THE GREEK FATHERS. *James Marshall Campbell.*

GREEK BIOLOGY AND MEDICINE. *Henry Osborn Taylor.*

MATHEMATICS. *David Eugene Smith.*

LOVE OF NATURE AMONG THE GREEKS AND ROMANS. *H. R. Fairclough.*

ANCIENT WRITING AND ITS INFLUENCE. *B. L. Ullman.*

GREEK ART. *Arthur Fairbanks.*

ARCHITECTURE. *Alfred M. Brooks.*

ENGINEERING. *Alexander P. Gest.*

MODERN TRAITS IN OLD GREEK LIFE. *Charles Burton Gulick.*

ROMAN PRIVATE LIFE. *Walton Brooks McDaniel.*

GREEK AND ROMAN FOLKLORE. *William Reginald Halliday.*

ANCIENT EDUCATION. *J. F. Dobson.*